OVERBURDENED SCHOOL-GOING CHILDREN

About the Author

Rashmi Pramanik (*b.* 1975) is a faculty in Anthropology at the Sambalpur University. She earned her Ph.D. in Anthropology from the Sambalpur University in June 2005. She topped the merit list in the M.Phil Anthropology Examination in 1999. Dr. Pramanik has to her credit half-a-dozen papers, all published in peer-reviewed journals. She has participated in a number of national and international conferences.

OVERBURDENED SCHOOL-GOING CHILDREN

Rashmi Pramanik

CONCEPT PUBLISHING COMPANY, NEW DELHI-110059

Cataloging in Publication Data—DK
Courtesy: D.K. Agencies (P) Ltd. <docinfo@dkagencies.com>

Pramanik, Rashmi, 1975-
Overburdened school-going children / Rashmi Pramanik.
p. ; cm.
Originally presented as the author's thesis (Ph. D.)—Sambalpur University, 2005.
Study conducted at Sambalpur City of Orissa State, India.
Includes bibliographical references (p.)
Includes index.
ISBN 8180693783

1. High school students—India—Sambalpur. 2. Overpressure (Education). I. Title.

DDC 373.180 954 133 22

ISBN : 81-8069-378-3

First Published 2007

Published and Printed by
Ashok Kumar Mittal
Concept Publishing Company
A/15-16, Commercial Block, Mohan Garden
New Delhi-110059 (India)

Phones : 25351460, 25351794
Fax : 091-11-25357103
Email : publishing@conceptpub.com

Dedicated to
my
Loving Parents

Acknowledgements

With due reverence, I express my deep sense of gratitude to my research supervisor Prof. D.K.Behera, Head, Department of Anthropology, Sambalpur University for his stimulating guidance and continuous encouragement throughout the investigation which enabled me to bring this study to its present shape. I am highly indebted to him for the valuable time he has spared for the completion of my work.

I take this opportunity to thank Prof. P.N. Sahu, Dr. P. Panda, Dr. R.K. Chaudhury and Dr. S.S. Guru for their constructive suggestions at different stages of my work.

I owe special thanks to Sr. Maurice, Principal, St. Joseph's Convent High School; Mr. Shantiraj Pandey, Principal, Madnabati Central Public School; Mr. Satya Nanda Rout, Headmaster, Chandra Sekhar Behera Zilla School and Mrs. Jayashree Dash, Headmistress, Municipal Girls' High School who helped me a lot throughout the period of data collection in their respective schools.

I shall fail in my duty if I do not extend my thanks to all my respondents (primary and secondary) who provided me with the required information for the present study quite happily and wilfully.

I would like to thank Mr. Rajib Das and Mr. Sanjit Das (Raj Computers), A.N. Guha Lane, Sambalpur for their help and sincere co-operation in converting the manuscript into a neat computerized script. The work would not have achieved its present shape without the timely support of Mr. Arun Kumar Basa, the computer expert of Sambalpur University.

I lack words to express my inmost feelings for my loving parents who provided me constant help and encouragement. Without their co-operation it would have been impossible on my part to complete this work successfully.

Last but not the least, I offer a special gratitude to my brother Er. Alok Pramanik, Sister-in-law Er. Nabanita Pramanik and nephew Rajeev Pramanik who have been constant source of inspiration for me. They stood as a moral support boosting me all through the study making my effort successful.

Rashmi Pramanik

Contents

List of Tables, Graphs, Charts and Plates

Tables

Graphs

Charts

Plates

1

Introduction

Childhood is a social phenomenon. It is so in the sense that every society crystallizes its own set of norms, rules and regulations, which dictate its attitudes towards the category of its members defined as children. The most prominent characteristics of a child, is that s/he is not (yet) an adult. S/he is often regarded as "not-yet-person", "not-yet-knowing", "not-yet-responsible", etc. In other words, s/he is viewed not as "human being" but as "human becoming". S/he is helpless, defenceless and dependent on adults during childhood. S/he requires care and protection not only from the parents but also from other members of the society.

Childhood is a period of preparation, a period of "still-not-being-able to and of no participation". It means that children are not supposed to act autonomously but that their actions are to a large extent directed, because children are by definition seen as those, who still have to learn to become useful members of society (Hungerland, 1999: 65). As the child grows into adolescence and is no longer a dependant child, the parents demand that s/he acts his/her age and try to confirm to adult standards of behaviour.

Children[1] are treated as marginal people whose activities and experiences matter less than those of adults. For many children of contemporary societies "the dominating feature of childhood is that of powerlessness and lack of control over what happens to them" (Lansdown, 1994: 34). Socially marginalized childhood[2] restricts children's activities to "child-specific places and child-specific ways" (Bardy, 1994: 307). The activities of children are strictly scheduled in time. Further "each kind of activity has its own adult leadership" (Nasman, 1994: 182). Children fail to reach public as a social category and to establish their own existence as a distinct social entity.

There is a trite segment of horticultural folklore which defines a weed as being "any plant that is growing in the wrong place". This is instructive of our understanding of the location of children. Children either occupy designated spaces, that is they are placed, as in nurseries or schools or they are conspicuous by their inappropriate or precocious invasion of adult territory. In terms of social space children are sited, insulated and distanced, and their very gradual emergence into wider, adult space is by accident, by degrees, as an award or as part of a gradualist rite de-passage. The particular nature of children is separate, it clearly and distinctly sets them apart from adults.

Children are one of the categories of people that are commonly denied to have "competence", even if depending upon the sphere of activity they acquire some decisional authority over their own lives before they come of age in a legalistic sense. The act of judging children "incompetent" severely restricts their autonomy to consent to or refuse matters affecting their lives (Mortier, 1997: 99). Now "voices have been heard emphasizing that children are first and foremost human beings and therefore, our relationship with them has to be based on respect for them as people" (Verhellen, 1994: 7). They "must be seen as active in the construction and determination of their own social lives, the lives of those around them and of the society in which they live" (James and Prout, 1997: 8). In other words, they must be looked upon as subjects and agents of their own construction, indeed as co-constructors of childhood and society.

Each child has certain rights that are of great importance. However, the rights of children are an abstract and legalistic concept. It does not help children until it is put into practice (Gross and Gross, 1977: 6). In reality, they have little opportunities to develop their potentials as they are steamrollered into areas, which are not of their inclinations and to levels which they have difficulty in attaining. They are protected from physical harm and their intellectual potentials are stretched to the limits and, may be beyond but the "right to rest and leisure, to engage in play and recreational activities appropriate to the age of the child and to participate freely in cultural life and the art is taken away from them" (UNICEF, 1992: 12). The development of a wholesome person with good physical health, emotional maturity and stable personality is thereby in doubt. Countless children in our contemporary societies have advanced almost directly from infancy into adulthood and if they ever-experienced childhood, it is only a fleeting stage. Children of contemporary societies are overburdened.

Today no society is considered to be complete without a school. It is here that imparting instruction in certain subjects and also training him in other works of life bring about the development of the personality of the child. Educational system represents the fundamental structural force of modern childhood. The educational system structures children's life through time spent in the school, the amount of homework, teacher attitude, course structure, etc.

The school is not only about learning facts and figures. The UN Convention on the Rights of the Child (hereafter CRC) expresses views about the spirit in the school and the values to be taught. The pedagogic methods should be administered in a manner consistent with the child's human dignity and in conformity with the present Convention (Article 28: 2). The UN committee interprets this to mean that corporal punishment should not be allowed in schools. The education should aim at developing the child's personality, talents and mental and physical abilities to the fullest potential. It should prepare the child for a responsible life in a free society, in the spirit of understanding, peace, tolerance, equality of sexes, and friendship among all people. Respect for human rights is mentioned specifically in Article 29. Article 31 covers the right of the child to rest, leisure and play.

This recognizes, clearly and explicitly, the important roles that children play in society, and their capacity to participate in society and to enjoy defined civil-political rights[3] that go much further than just their protection and other basis needs. The UN Convention on the Rights of the Child has established as fundamental need to inform children of their rights so that they know them, understand them and can insist that they are met. Subsequent other documents stress the need to promote child participation[4] and also that of parents and children, as a way of developing their sense of community responsibility and making citizenship a real experience for them.

The present day competitive and expanding school system contributes heavily to the development of an educational ideology of upbringing. It can be argued that the character of children's education as a basic investment in the future implies that education may be interpreted as work. The expanding educational system dominating children's day to an ever-increasing extent represents the child labour of the post-industrial society (Field, 1995: 51). There is at present a tendency to crowd the syllabus of each subject with too many facts and often of little significance. Our curriculum makers at the school levels are more concerned with the logical and scientific demands of the subject than the needs, the psychology and the interests of the learners. We should design a curriculum of change, not merely a "changing curriculum".

The new working child is the school child (Qvortrup, 1987: 15). Parents and teachers press the child to excel in the world of competition, particularly in academic pursuits. Indeed, this concern is evident in all cultures that value academic accomplishment. Endeavour made to accelerate children's acquisition of academic skills begins, for many, soon after birth. Academic training that begins at four years of age is considered to be too late. Schools like to have "good results" and they know that ambitious parents will goad their children into achieving good examination results. Thus, all educational practices are, in some sense non-human because they presuppose that a real match between educational measures and children's needs does exist. Such presuppositions are made by adults completely ignoring the children's views. Thus children's needs are reified and naturalized (Castro, 1996: 76). So the adult conspiracies against childhood thrive. School has further institutionalized the separation of the children from the society, confirming upon them a separate identity: their proper place is in the classroom.

The short-sightedness regarding children has reached epidemic proportions. The future looms so large in the mental horizons of educated parents, that the present is totally engulfed. The present becomes a means to an end, the end being the future. The future has no trace of happiness or compassion as objectives to be attained or traits to be cultivated. Child's future as envisaged by parents is a comfortable life, success, money, etc. The importance of these aims is blow-up by the parents out of proportion. The current definition of "comfort" could not even have been imagined three decades ago; it is a conglomeration of consumer-durables, ready-to-eat foods, state-of-the-art information technology and citizenship of a developed country. Success, to start with, is academics: ranks, stars, medals and the works, soon followed by career options. Pushing children towards these objectives also means putting them into straitjackets at various times in the childhood span. In the process, the educational system is a willing partner. It appears that numerous parents are bent on hot housing their children in attempts to produce geniuses.

Parents often feel intimidated by teachers and are haunted by the memories of childhood school experiences that were perhaps not pleasant. Parents often do not know what questions to ask or how much to interfere in the school life of their children. Teachers sometimes lead them to feel that they are on opposite tracks when it comes to the welfare of their children, many fail to realize that home circumstances are sometimes beyond their control. Rather than looking at each and blaming the school or the home for the problems of the child, both parents and teachers need to be more tolerant of each other and to work together to help the children. Exposing them to adults' anxieties and troubles is unloading adults' problems and placing them on the child's young shoulders.

The demarcation between childhood and adulthood should be very well defined so that children are not deemed as miniature version of adults. They have their own distinctive identity with their peculiar characteristics and needs. Pushing them to grow up faster intellectually, socially and psychologically will cripple them in their development and rob them of their childhood. From the point of view of adults, children should remain secluded in homes and in schools because the world at large can be dangerous for them (Castro, 2000: 139). Children are thus excluded from adult world. Children are constantly told, "it is for their good", and generally an attempt on the part of the children to ask for a re-definition of parental authorities is treated like a freedom slogan in an occupied country. The quality of childhood has clearly deteriorated. Aries (1962) concludes that the family and the school are responsible for removing the child from the adult society.

Review of Literature

Overviews of literature reveals that most of the existing studies in this area are fragmentary and thereby do not appreciably add to our understanding on the problem at hand. Mention may be made here about a few from the available literature.

Cohen (1996 : 77) asserts that the definition of children's problem is undergoing transformation. It is high time that children should participate in making decisions affecting them. Their legitimate human rights now include not only care and protection but also adequate opportunity for development of their potential.

Pillai (1979: 56) investigated the organizational and administrative factors, which affect the achievement of pupils in secondary schools. The study aimed at finding out the non-instructional factors affecting the achievement of candidates appearing for the secondary school certificate examinations in Kerala.

Bremback (1966: 3) discusses about the environment of the school. He stated "going to school is common experience for children around the world". Though education is a universal phenomenon, the common and uncommon experiences in school reflect much about education, the social setting and environment where the students live.

Thompson (1969: 180) focused on the discipline of the students. He laid emphasis on the due "reward" for the disciplined students and "punishment" for the erring ones, which would contribute towards healthy management of education on the children. It is a fact that when reward recognizes ability, aptitude and talent, it positively contributes to the cause of education.

Greenberg (1989: 61) emphasizes that the parent's presence in the school itself is helpful, it is not the amount of time parents spend at school, but rather how respected they feel in school-family relationship.

Epstein (1995: 732) recommends that school-parent involvement includes parents support in education, volunteering activities, involvement in school-related learning activities at home, collaboration with the community and the establishment of better communication and relation among students, parents and school staff.

Srivastav (1985: 36) discusses the parent-child relationship. He states, socially a child at the first place is affiliated to family and its parents. So the parent-child relationship plays an important role in the overall development of the child and it is true for any rural or urban society.

Baldwin (1979: 313) in his study shows the correlation between parents' behaviour and personality of their children. His research suggests that democratic living practiced in the home has a great affect on children's behaviour in the school. Children from democratic homes are more active, more socially outgoing and higher in intellectual curiosity, originality and constructiveness.

Phearman (1969: 405) in his study discusses that there is a direct relationship between the education of the parents and the probability of their children's interest for higher studies. Thus the forces that determine the high school students' interest in education come primarily from his parents and secondarily from those forces such as peer groups and teachers.

Ahhunawallia (1985: 39) has outlined the main determining factors for the educational achievement of the children. These are parents' education, economic status and size of the family.

Sachidananda (1989: 145) agrees to the fact that the inter-relation between education and the institution of family is one of considerable importance. The resources at the disposal of the family as well as the outlook of its elders towards education become crucial determinant of the educational attainments of the members of younger generation.

Chinnapan (1987: 29) is of opinion that the parental occupational level and educational attainment of children are closely associated. Besides, family environment holds an important position for the educational attainments of the child. Because family is a place of secured living and learning for every child.

OECD (1997: 48) highlights the role of parents in helping their children in homework. The latest figures collected for OECD's education indicators project suggest that about 75 per cent of primary pupils go to schools that regularly engage parents in actively supporting their children's learning at home.

Olmos (1983: 127) recommends that all students regardless of background can benefit from well-designed homework. Studies of migrant children's education and cultural development emphasize that homework is beneficial when it is supervised either by teachers or parents.

Heredia (1992: 247) has focused on the integration of community within society, the school within the community, the pupil within the school and the teacher within the educational system.

The above review of literature on school-going children reveals that even today there exist only a few comprehensive and systematic studies highlighting the life of school-going children. The existing studies further do not give a clear picture of the overburdened children. Hence the present study is significant both for analytical and policy-related reasons.

Methodology

The study views that the collective images of children are always grounded in a particular cultural setting and therefore childhood is a "social construct". Here children is taken as "unit of observation" and childhood as the "unit of analysis" in different settings.

Universe

The study is conducted among the school-going children covering four different schools of Sambalpur city. The four high schools selected (out of a total number of 18 high schools) for the present study are: St. Joseph's Convent High School, Madnabati Central Public School, Chandra Sekhar Behera Zilla School, Municipal Girls' High School.

Two of those are English medium schools and the other two are Oriya medium schools. Our sample schools to a large extent represent the all India picture, as one finds schools of these types all over the urban India. The students of the sample schools are exposed to three different types of course curriculum, viz. Indian Certificate Secondary Examination (ICSE), Central Board of Secondary Education (CBSE) and High School Certificate Examination (HSC) (Chart 1).

Chart 1: Distribution of sample students in terms of their course affiliation [N=240]

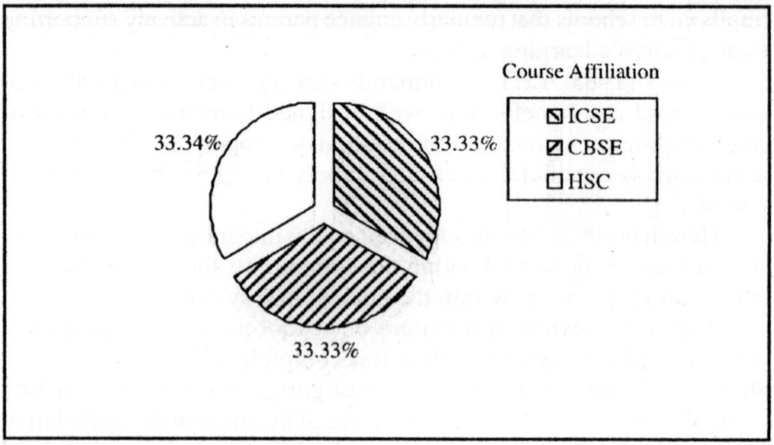

Sample Size and Sample Unit

Students from class VI to class X are selected as the primary respondents of the study. They fall in the age group of less than 12[5] and more than 15[6]. Both male and female students are included in our sample. A random sampling technique is adopted for this study. The respondents are selected by lottery method. The sample students are selected from the class attendance registers. A total number of 240 children constituted the sample of the present study. Of the 240 children, 80 (33.33%) are taken from ICSE school, 80 (33.33%) from CBSE School and 80 (33.34%) from HSC school (40 from Boys' High school and 40 from Girls' High School). A total number of 16 (6.67%) students are selected from each standard of which 8 (3.33%) are boys and 8 (3.33%) are girls. (Table 1.1). This is applicable for St. Joseph's Convent High School and Madnabati Central Public School as they are co-educational schools. But in the case of Chandra Sekhar

Table 1.1: Distribution of sample students of the schools in terms of their sex and educational standard [N=240]

Educational Standard	*Sex*	*Sample Schools*				*Total*
		SJCHS (ICSE)	*MCPS (CBSE)*	*CSBZS (HSC)*	*MGHS (HSC)*	
Class-VI	M	08	08	08	—	24
	F	08	08	—	08	24
Class-VII	M	08	08	08	—	24
	F	08	08	—	08	24
Class-VIII	M	08	08	08	—	24
	F	08	08	--	08	24
Class-IX	M	08	08	08	—	24
	F	08	08	—	08	24
Class-X	M	08	08	08	—	24
	F	08	08	—	08	24
Total		80	80	40	40	240

Behera Zilla School and Municipal Girls' High School only 8 students are selected from each standard. Hence in a total number of 120 male students and 120 female students are selected for the present study. The sample students are then divided into a systematic break-up of three age groups, *i.e.* less than 12, 13-14 and more than 15 years of age (Chart 2).

Chart 2: Distribution of sample students in terms of their age groups [N=240]

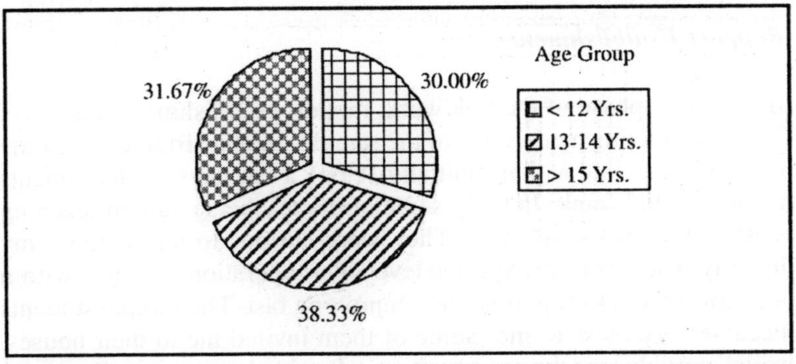

The school-going children studying between class VI and class X are the primary respondents. The parents and the teachers of the primary respondents constituted the secondary respondents. Interviews are conducted in order to assess the attitude and behaviour of parents towards their children, their expectation from the children and their opinion on the present course curriculum, examination pattern, administration of the school, etc.

Methods of Data Collection

Instead of depending on any particular method, the study has used different methods for data collection. Relevant information is gathered with the help of three different sets of interview schedules. Of the three, one interview schedule is prepared for the sample students, another for their parents and the last one for the teachers. Apart from that an interview guide and an observation schedule are also prepared. Both participant and non-participant observation methods are employed for data collection. Besides these techniques, case study method is also used to supplement our analysis. Secondary data are collected from different sources such as official records, statistical handbooks and published and unpublished literature. Data regarding the city are collected from the Municipality and Town Planning Offices.

It approximately took a time period of eight months for the completion of the fieldwork. The data and information have been collected, analyzed and presented in the form of bi-variate and multi-variate tables. Cross tabulations are done wherever it is necessary. The qualitative aspect of the information has been presented in a descriptive form. However, all the collected data are analysed with the help of computer software packages.

Rapport Establishment

In the early phase of the fieldwork, rapport establishment was done. The first meeting made some of the sample students frightened. Some did not co-operate with me initially. It took a few days for the students to be free and frank. Initially some of the teachers and non-teaching staffs were also suspicious. They were curious to know about my identity. There was no expected level of co-operation. Anyhow within a couple of weeks things started improving fast. The sample students became very close to me. Some of them invited me to their houses, which provided me the opportunity to talk with their parents. Gradually the principal, teachers and other staffs became familiar with me. They understood the purpose of my research and extended their possible co-operation. This made it easier for me to examine their attitude and expectations and also to study the relationship among the parents, teachers and students.

Objectives

The major objectives of the study are :—

(i) To study the functioning of the sample schools;
(ii) To critically examine the course curriculum of the sample schools;
(iii) To analyze the activities of the students at school as well as the teachers' attitude towards and expectation from the children;
(iv) To discuss different activities of the students at home and the expectation of their parents from them; and
(v) To record the voices of the children regarding their experiences at school and home.

The Study Area

Sambalpur is situated in the western part of Orissa. In the year 1993, Jharsuguda, Deogarh and Bargarh were separated from the undivided Sambalpur, thereby forming an independent small Sambalpur district. It extends over an area of 6657sq. kms. It is bounded by Sundargarh district in the north, Jharsuguda district in the northwest, Bargarh district in the west and Subarnapur district in the southwest. Angul district lies in the southeast part whereas Deogarh district is situated in the eastern region of Sambalpur. At present Sambalpur comprises a total number of three sub-divisions, four tahasils, nine blocks, and hundred thirty-three gram panchayats. According to the 2001 census, the total population of Sambalpur is 9,28,889. The density of population is 140/sq.km. The study area is in a tropical monsoon region. The yearly average rainfall is 1527 mm.

The city of Sambalpur had its prominence as an important centre of trade and power ever since the mid-seventeen century till the end of British hegemony on Indian soil. As far as religion is concerned the city is a storehouse of temples, mosques, and churches symbolizing its rich heritage of art, culture and universal brotherhood. Sambalpur has remained a pivotal centre of educational growth with a great network of educational institutions. It provides better educational facilities to its inhabitants irrespective of caste and sex. There are 18 High Schools in Sambalpur city. Besides, there are two co-educational

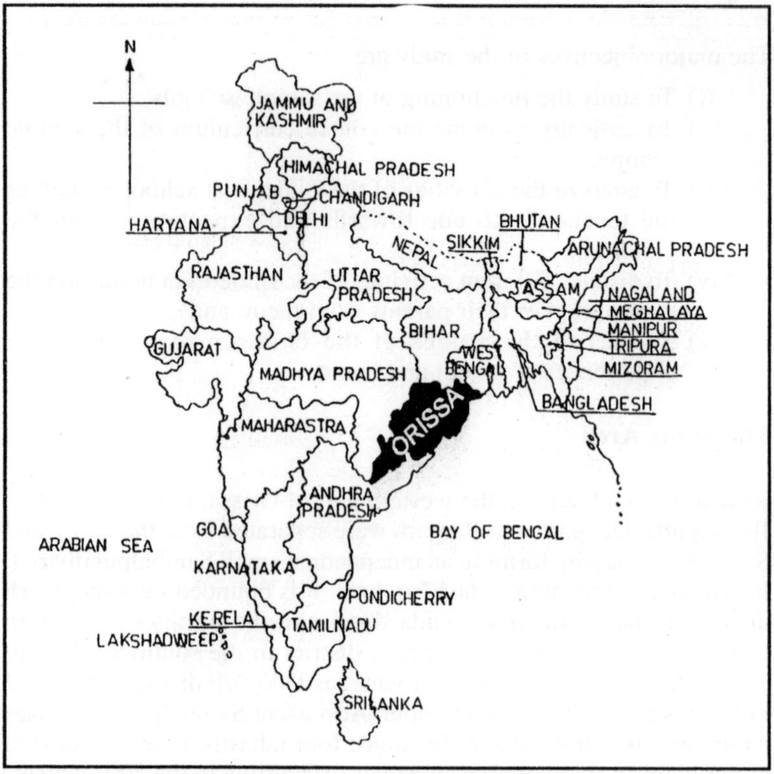

Map 1: Showing Orissa in India

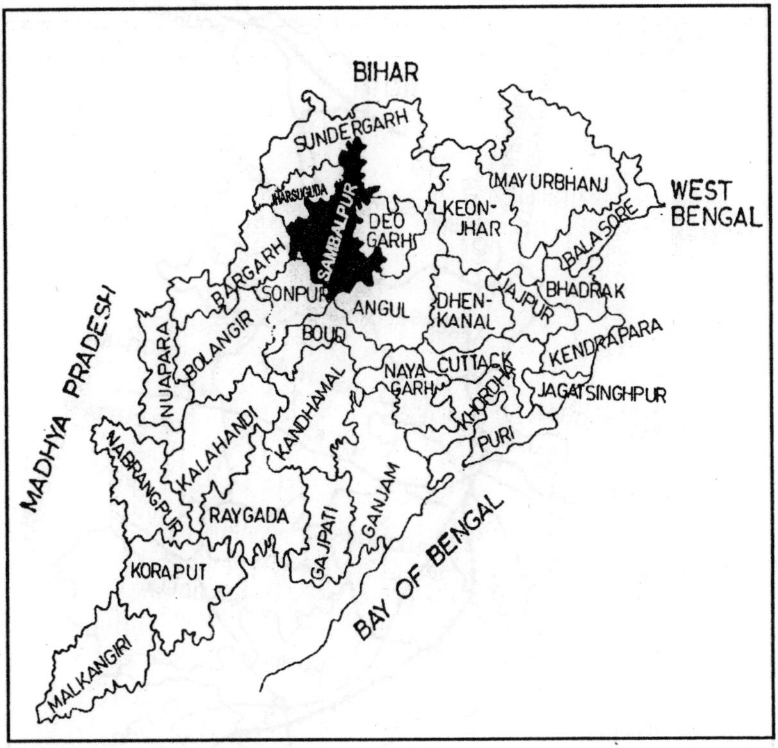

Map 2: Showing Sambalpur District in Orissa

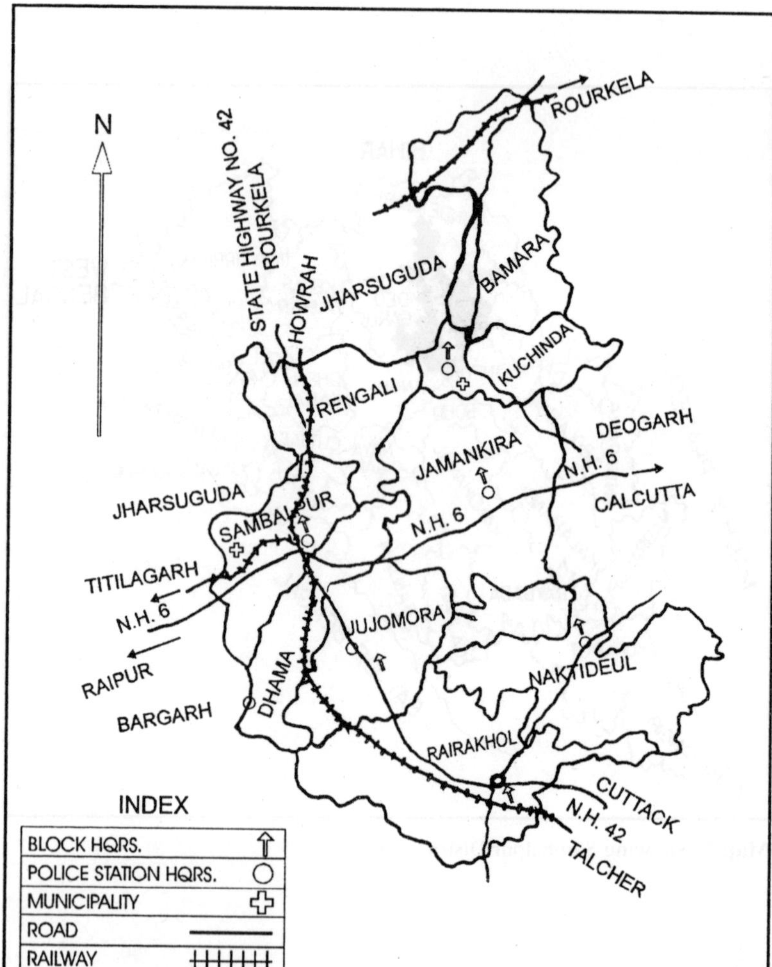

Map 3: Showing Sambalpur District

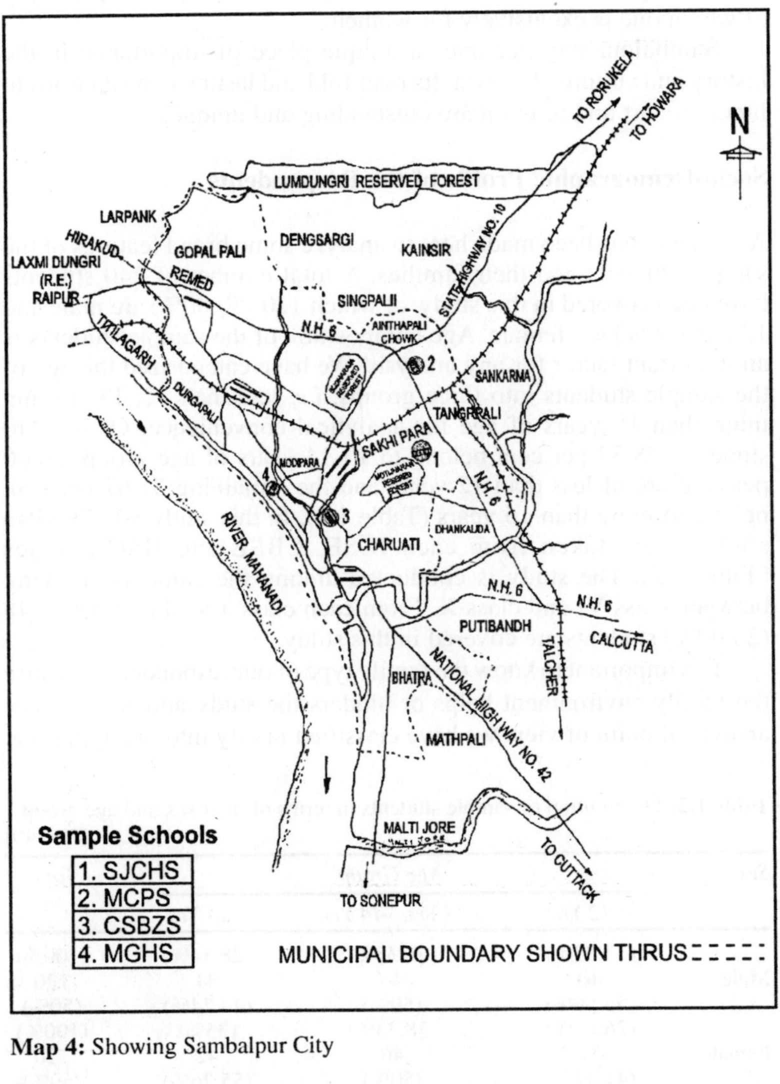

Map 4: Showing Sambalpur City

schools, namely Central School and a St. Joseph's Convent School. In recent time a number of Nursery Schools have also come up. As far as college education is concerned, the city has six general colleges, of which one is exclusively for women.

Sambalpur city occupies a unique place of importance in the history and culture of Orissa. Its manifold and lasting contributions to literature, art and religion are outstanding and unique.

Socio-Demographic Profile of the Respondents

An attempt has been made here to analyze some broad features of the sample students and their families. A total number of 240 students have been covered in this study, of which 120 (50.00%) are male and 120 (50.00%) are female. Age composition of the sample students is an important factor for any analysis. We have categorized the age of the sample students into three groups, *i.e.* less than 12, 13, 14 and more than 15 years of age for analytical convenience. Of the 240 students, 38.33 per cent belong to 13-14 years of age group, 30.00 per cent are of less than 12 years and the remaining 31.67 per cent belong to more than 15 years (Table 1.2). In this study 80 (33.33%) students are taken from each ICSE, CBSE and HSC courses (Table 1.3). The study is conducted among the students studying between class VI and class X. From each class a total number of 48 (20.00%) students are covered in this study.

It is important to know the family type of our respondents because the family environment helps or hinders the study atmosphere. For analytical point of view we have classified family into two types, *i.e.*

Table 1.2: Distribution of sample students in terms of their sex and age group

[N=240]

Sex	*Age Group*			*Total*
	< 12 Yrs.	*13 Yrs. –14 Yrs.*	*> 15 Yrs.*	
Male	(33.33%) 40 (55.56%)	(38.33%) 46 (50%)	(28.34%) 34 (44.74%)	(100%) 120 (50%)
Female	(26.67%) 32 (44.44%)	(38.33%) 46 (50%)	(35%) 42 (55.26%)	(100%) 120 (50%)
Total	(30%) 72 (100%)	(38.33%) 92 (100%)	(31.67%) 76 (100%)	(100%) 240 (100%)

Table 1.3: Distribution of sample students in terms of their course affiliation and sex [N=240]

Sex	*Course Affiliation*			*Total*
	ICSE	*CBSE*	*HSC*	
Male	(33.33%) 40 (50%)	(33.33%) 40 (50%)	(33.34%) 40 (50%)	(100%) 120 (50%)
Female	(33.33%) 40 (50%)	(33.33%) 40 (50%)	(33.34%) 40 (50%)	(100%) 120 (50%)
Total	(33.33%) 80 (100%)	(33.33%) 80 (100%)	(33.34%) 80 (100%)	(100%) 240 (100%)

Table 1.4: Distribution of sample students in terms of their course affiliation and age group [N=240]

Age Group	*Course Affiliation*			*Total*
	ICSE	*CBSE*	*HSC*	
< 12 Yrs.	(27.78%) 20 (25%)	(31.94%) 23 (28.75%)	(40.28%) 29 (36.25%)	(100%) 72 (30%)
13-14 Yrs.	(34.78%) 32 (40%)	(34.78%) 32 (40%)	(30.44%) 28 (35%)	(100%) 92 (38.33%)
> 15 Yrs.	(36.84%) 28 (35%)	(32.89%) 25 (31.25%)	(30.26%) 23 (28.75%)	(100%) 76 (31.67%)
Total	(33.33%) 80 (100%)	(33.33%) 80 (100%)	(33.34%) 80 (100%)	(100%) 240 (100%)

nuclear (a family having parents and unmarried children) and extended family (a family consisting of more than one nuclear family) (Chart 3). Of the total sample students, more than half (*i.e.* 55.00%)

Chart 3: Distribution of sample students in terms of their family type [N=240]

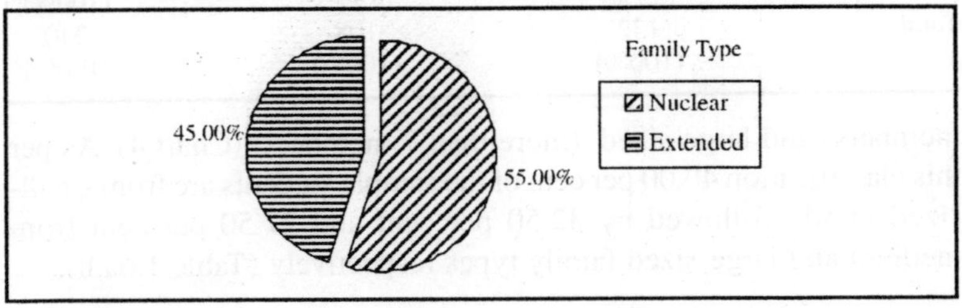

are members of nuclear family and 45.00 per cent are from extended family background (Table 1.5a,b). We have classified the families of the sample students into three broad categories on the basis of their sizes, *i.e.* small-sized (less than 4 members), medium-sized (5-7

Table 1.5a: Distribution of sample students in terms of their family type and sex [N=240]

Sex	*Family Type*		*Total*
	Nuclear	*Extended*	
Male	(50%) 60 (45.45%)	(50%) 60 (55.56%)	(100%) 120 (50%)
Female	(60%) 72 (54.55%)	(40%) 48 (44.44%)	(100%) 120 (50%)
Total	(55%) 132 (100%)	(45%) 108 (100%)	(100%) 240 (100%)

Table 1.5b: Distribution of sample students in terms of their family type and course affiliation [N=240]

Course Affiliation	*Family Type*		*Total*
	Nuclear	*Extended*	
ICSE	(67.5%) 54 (40.91%)	(32.5%) 26 (24.07%)	(100%) 80 (33.33%)
CBSE	(46.25%) 37 (28.03%)	(53.75%) 43 (39.81%)	(100%) 80 (33.33%)
HSC	(51.25%) 41 (31.06%)	(48.75%) 39 (36.12%)	(100%) 80 (33.34%)
Total	(55%) 132 (100%)	(45%) 108 (100%)	(100%) 240 (100%)

members) and large-sized (more than 7 members) (Chart 4). As per this classification 40.00 per cent of the sample students are from small-sized family followed by 32.50 per cent and 27.50 per cent from medium and large-sized family types respectively (Table 1.6a,b).

Chart 4: Distribution of sample students in terms of their family size [N=240]

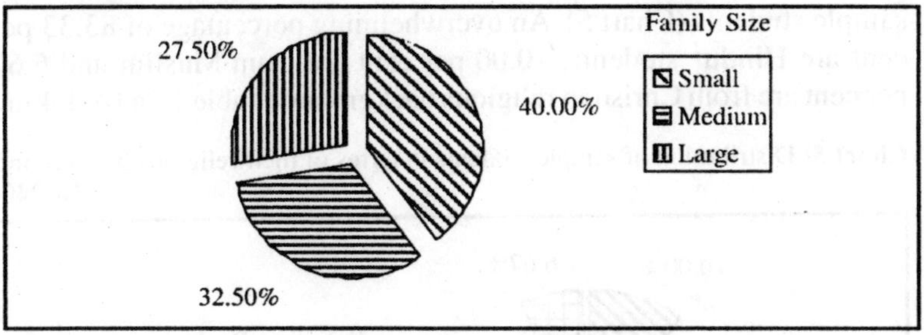

Table 1.6a: Distribution of sample students in terms of their family size and sex [N=240]

Sex	*Family Size*			*Total*
	Small	*Medium*	*Large*	
Male	(46.67%)	(30%)	(23.33%)	(100%)
	56	36	28	120
	(58.33%)	(46.15%)	(42.42%)	(50%)
Female	(33.33%)	(35%)	(31.67%)	(100%)
	40	42	38	120
	(41.67%)	(53.85%)	(57.58%)	(50%)
Total	(40%)	(32.5%)	(27.5%)	(100%)
	96	78	66	240
	(100%)	(100%)	(100%)	(100%)

Table 1.6b: Distribution of sample students in terms of their family size and course affiliation [N=240]

Course Affiliation	*Family Size*			*Total*
	Small	*Medium*	*Large*	
	(40%)	(36.25%)	(23.75%)	(100%)
ICSE	32	29	19	80
	(33.33%)	(37.18%)	(28.79%)	(33.33%)
	(53.75%)	(31.25%)	(15%)	(100%)
CBSE	43	25	12	80
	(44.8%)	(32.05%)	(18.18%)	(33.33%)
	(26.25%)	(30%)	(43.75%)	(100%)
HSC	21	24	35	80
	(21.88%)	(30.77%)	(53.03%)	(33.34%)
	(40%)	(32.5%)	(27.5%)	(100%)
Total	96	78	66	240
	(100%)	(100%)	(100%)	(100%)

An analysis has been made on the religious affiliation of the sample students (Chart 5). An overwhelming percentage of 83.33 per cent are Hindu[7] students, 10.00 per cent are from Muslim and 6.67 per cent are from Christian religious background (Table 1.7a,b). Taking

Chart 5: Distribution of sample students in terms of their religious background [N=240]

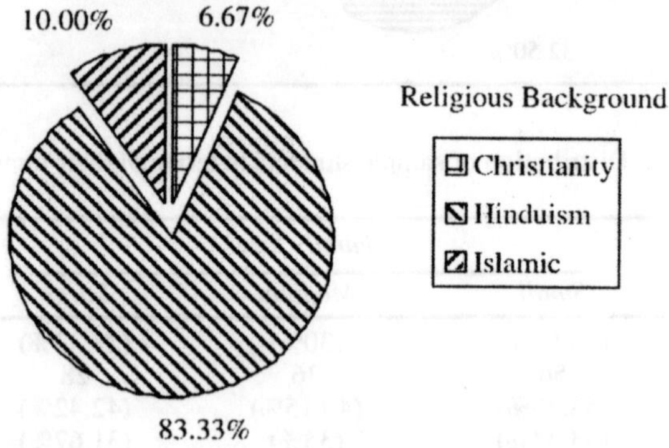

Table 1.7a: Distribution of sample students in terms of their religious background and sex [N=240]

Sex	*Religious Background*			*Total*
	Christianity	*Hinduism*	*Islamic*	
Male	(5%) 06 (37.5%)	(87.5%) 105 (52.5%)	(7.5%) 09 (37.5%)	(100%) 120 (50%)
Female	(8.33%) 10 (63.5%)	(79.17%) 95 (47.5%)	(12.5%) 15 (62.5%)	(100%) 120 (50%)
Total	(6.67%) 16 (100%)	(83.33%) 200 (100%)	(10%) 24 (100%)	(100%) 240 (100%)

into account the monthly income of the parents, the economic conditions of the sample students have been categorized into three groups, *i.e.* low-income group, middle-income group and high-income group. The economic condition of the family mainly depends on the employment status of the parents (Chart 6). Of the 240 sample students,

Table 7b: Distribution of sample students in terms of their religious background and course affiliation [N=240]

Course Affiliation	*Religious Background*			*Total*
	Christianity	*Hinduism*	*Islamic*	
ICSE	(10%) 08 (50%)	(77.5%) 62 (31%)	(12.5%) 10 (41.67%)	(100%) 80 (33.33%)
CBSE	(6.25%) 05 (31.25%)	(82.5%) 66 (33%)	(11.25%) 09 (33.5%)	(100%) 80 (33.33%)
HSC	(3.75%) 03 (18.75%)	(90%) 72 (36%)	(6.25%) 05 (20.83%)	(100%) 80 (33.34%)
Total	(6.67%) 16 (100%)	(83.33%) 200 (100%)	(10%) 24 (100%)	(100%) 240 (100%)

Chart 6: Distribution of sample students in terms of their economic standard [N=240]

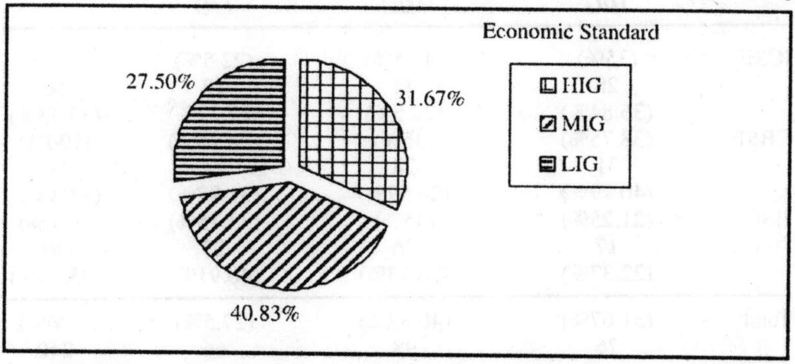

76 (31.67%) are from high-income bracket whereas the corresponding figures for middle-income group and low-income group are 98 (40.83%) and 66 (27.50%) respectively (Table 1.8a,b).

Significance

Though there exists a great deal of literature on children and childhood in India, yet a few studies exclusively deal with the various problems encountered by the school-going children at the micro-level. The present study deals with the overburdened school-going children of Sambalpur city of Western Orissa. Besides stating the general problems

Table 1.8a: Distribution of sample students in terms of their economic standard of the family and sex [N=240]

Sex	*Economic Standard of the Family*			*Total*
	HIG	*MIG*	*LIG*	
Male	(29.17%) 35 (46.05%)	(48.33%) 58 (59.18%)	(22.5%) 27 (40.91%)	(100%) 120 (50%)
Female	(34.17%) 41 (53.95%)	(33.33%) 40 (40.82%)	(32.5%) 39 (59.09%)	(100%) 120 (50%)
Total	(31.67%) 76 (100%)	(40.83%) 98 (100%)	(27.5%) 66 (100%)	(100%) 240 (100%)

Table 1.8b: Distribution of sample students in terms of their economic standard of the family and course affiliation [N=240]

Course Affiliation	*Economic Standard of the Family*			*Total*
	HIG	*MIG*	*LIG*	
ICSE	(35%) 28 (36.84%)	(42.5%) 34 (22.5%)	(22.5%) 18 (27.27%)	(100%) 80 (33.33%)
CBSE	(38.75%) 31 (40.79%)	(35%) 28 (28.57%)	(26.25%) 21 (31.82%)	(100%) 80 (33.33%)
HSC	(21.25%) 17 (22.37%)	(45%) 36 (36.73%)	(33.75%) 27 (40.91%)	(100%) 80 (33.34%)
Total	(31.67%) 76 (100%)	(40.83%) 98 (100%)	(27.5%) 66 (100%)	(100%) 240 (100%)

of the school-going children it focuses on those specific problems for which the school-going children feel physically and mentally overburdened. It is argued that there is a special need for the study of overburdened school-going children as a separate category and also as an important section of the population for a social investigation.

The present study is picked up with a view to explore the social reality regarding the overburdened school-going children, which will open a way for further research. More research is needed to illuminate the darkness that surrounds the school-going children in our contemporary society. The present study is not enough to provide adequate and comprehensive information on various aspects of the problem. However, it is hoped that the limitations of this study will necessitate new research undertakings by scholars to fill in the existing gaps.

Organization of Data

The data for the study have been organized in seven chapters. The second chapter provides an overview of the theories and concepts of children and childhood. The following chapter gives an account of the functioning of the sample schools. Chapter IV examines the course curriculum and syllabus of the sample schools.

The fifth chapter makes an analysis of the various activities of the students at school. It also deals with the attitude of the teachers' towards the students. The next chapter explicitly highlights participation of the school-going children in various activities at home. It also analyzes the high expectations of the parents from their children. The last chapter presents the concluding remarks of the findings. Finally, the study presents some case studies in addition to the tables, graphs/charts, maps, photographs and bibliography.

NOTES

1. The word "Children" is used throughout the text to refer to minors, *i.e.* UN Convention on the Rights of the child says, a child means every human being below the age of 18 years.
2. It reflects childhood through adults' eyes; it is produced by an adult society for an adult society. It means how childhood is positioned by the adult generation in an adult generation in an adult society.
3. Included among these rights are: freedom of religion; freedom of association and assembly; freedom of expression, including the right to be heard; and the right to privacy.
4. The term "child participation" is used as an umbrella term. Children's participation includes: the way children take part in the social division of labour and the way children's individual and social "voice" gets heard.
5. By less than 12 I mean the student who is less than or equal to 12 years of age studying in class VI.
6. I have used more than 15 to show the student who is either 15 years or more than that, studying in class X.
7. This also includes students from Sikh background.

2

Overburdened School-Going Children:
A Conceptual Framework

The child is active in its own right, not simply imitatively, but as an agent in its own construction and as naturally an agent as any adult, in the sense of agency that concerns the initiation of action by choice (Wartofsky, 1981: 199). The term "children" denotes not only "child" in the plural, but also the "incumbents" of the structural category "childhood". Children are persons and must, therefore, be treated as units of observation in the statistical sense and childhood is a category and a social status and must thus be dealt with as our unit of analysis.

The concept of the child is culture-bound. From the collective perspective, childhood should be described as that period of time in each person's life which society allocates for the process of training to become the kind of member that the society wants him/her to be. Thus, the phenomenon of childhood always exists and only the individuals who are experiencing childhood are constantly changing. During this period, different agencies of society are expected to ensure that the child will be transformed into an adult in accordance with the adult-image acceptable in that society. From an individual point of view, childhood is that period during which persons are subject to a set of rules and regulation unique to them and one that does not apply to members of other social categories. Moreover, childhood is a period in a person's life during which he/she is neither expected nor allowed to fully participate in various domains of social life. For example, children are excluded from the basic political activity in any democracy voting (Hughes, 1989: 42).

Children are human being, not only "human becoming". They have not only needs, a fact which is recognized, they have also interests, that may or may not be compatible with interests of other social groups or categories, and they are exposed to societal forces like other groups. At the same time children and childhood are influenced by external social forces in particular ways, exactly as other groups in our society are influenced in accordance with their status, their activities and how they are valued. Especially important, as far as politics is concerned, it is to ask how children's needs and interests are met in the midst of the ensemble of other (adult) interests, which on the one side have their own intrinsic purposes, on the other – and partly depending on these purposes – far from always concord with children's best interests.

In our modern technological societies children are born, for the most part, because they are wanted. By society, they are wanted in order to ensure the physical and social replacement of its members, and by their families; they are wanted for a variety of reasons, including that of their own continuation. However, not all children born are wanted. The wanted children are those that are physically healthy, mentally sound and "well brought up". These children do not just "happen," they have to be "made". If only certain children are wanted, then newborn babies can be regarded as the "raw material" out of which each of the various parties involved intends to create a "product" that will conform to its own ideals.

Children are allowed to participate only in marginal economic activities. There are severe limitations on the right of children to be employed and their rights as consumers are also restricted. Furthermore, children's personal freedom, including freedom of movement is quite limited [*e.g.* they are not allowed to be outside their own home after certain hours, nor are they allowed to be (left) unsupervised at home when considered too young]. At the same time, the child is expected to become an adult during the period of childhood, although s/he is restricted from experiencing fully those activities that define adulthood (Boocock, 1976: 421). It is mainly a better understanding of what we, all adults are doing in regard to children, and a more humble a awareness that what we are doing for children is, at the same time, what we are doing to children, while molding them to fulfil our own ideals.

Children in modern time are busy: "child energy is not frittered away in idle play or innocent enjoyment". Children work and even their free time is less and less free, because alongside with an "increased supervision and curricularization of children's lives", children's leisure experiences an "increased commoditization" (Qvortrup, 1994: 7). There has always been disagreement about where to place children – at least this was very much so a century ago when children changed their work from classical child labour to school labour. This history was about struggles between different sectors of society, for instance on the one side poor people, peasants, artisans who fought for keeping children as a labour force directly in production and manufacture; on the other side the eventually more powerful forces like industrialists, the labour movement, and the state which successfully struggled for bringing children to the schools, while on the fringe stood a diversity of child-savers who fuelled the battle with moral arguments. Each and everyone in this historical fight represented interests; now-a-days, when nobody objects against children's scholarization as such, the fronts have changed, but the struggle over childhood has not disappeared – it has only adopted new expressions. Children are beginning to be considered as full human beings, as persons, who deserve the very same treatment in statistics and social accounting as adults (Qvortrup, 1994: 12).

There are two important factors, which need to be highlighted in connection with children's labour – whether in terms of classical child labour or modern school labour – namely, firstly, that children are active, and that adult society counts on children's activities and secondly, that their labour has worth. While children's manual labour in 19th century Europe and in our days is recognized as a constructive activity, which has value, it is much harder for adults today to acknowledge that school labour is a valuable activity.

Marginalization

Social marginalization appears to be one of the dominant organizing characteristics. The relationship between adults and children is characterized at the societal level by "protection and exclusion". Children are placed in "waiting rooms", *i.e.* such child institutions as schools, to become adults under the guidance and supervision of adults. As a consequence of this social exclusion, the dependency of minors on adults has become deeper and longer. The difference between childhood and adulthood is perceived clearly, and children are set apart from the adult world so that they can grow up protected.

Children are marginalized (or excluded) in a society in which adulthood is thought of as being of paramount importance. The concept of "marginalization" seems to be pertinent, not only as to where it takes place, but also as to its nature (Qvortrup, 1994: 21). Marginalization is coupled with children's need for "protection". It is a convenient tool to protect the adult world against intrusion of children.

So marginalization may be protective, but it may also at the same time or alternatively be "paternalistic". Paternalism is the kind of power, which is exerted benevolently: in case, there is no reason to believe in anything but good intentions on the side of single adults, in particular parents, teachers, etc. actually, paternalistic arguments generally hold that those marginalized on paternalistic grounds are finally the beneficiaries of their exclusion, while the benefactors are burdened with responsibility and power.

Minority Group

The relationship between adulthood and childhood diverts the elements for categorizing childhood as a "minority group". In its classical definition a minority group is one, which is defined by its subordinate relationship to a dominant group (the adults); it is a "status, which carries with it the exclusion from full participation in the life of society" (Wirth, 1995: 347). There is not necessarily a contradiction between a class and a minority group—indeed a suppressed class will probably always be carrying minority status, but the concept of "class" is more demanding, in particular in its Marxian sense, because it presupposes both exploitative relations and class consciousness. In a different framework, however, Boulding has categorized children as objects of class action, which in her interpretation, refers to legal action taken with regard to any category of person, such as women, children, the elderly or specific ethnic or racial minorities, on the basis of membership in that category rather than on the basis of the individual situation or need (Boulding, 1999: 97).

Individuation

"Individuation" refers primarily to the tendency of the modern state and organizational system to treat the individual as the basic unit. Legal rights and responsibilities, taxation, and the allocation of social welfare benefits, are, to an increasing extent, applied to the individual, not the household (Frones, 1994: 147). The purpose of enhanced individuation is not to emphasize the uniqueness of the single individual, his/her "individuality", but to ensure that everyone has the same rights and obligations and to make control and support more efficient.

Children are exposed to a kind of collective judgments, while their individuality and personal capacities are ignored. Actually, this is a good example of "individuation", where bureaucratic convenience is preferred to at the cost of individual considerations.

Individualization

The process of "individualization" emphasizes that children are unique personalities, but, at the same time, places the responsibility for the personality development on the parents. This leads to paradoxes that cannot be ignored when considering the family as an institution and as social organization. It emphasizes on the individual as a psychological personality, but is not a response to bureaucratic needs. Children are identified, registered, evaluated and treated as individuals and as adult citizens (Nasman, 1994: 167).

When we speak of individuation and about children as a collectivity, children may be exposed to a process of "individualization", whereby we are rather thinking of a breakup from their families although perhaps more as an empirical reality than ideologically.

Institutionalization

The "institutionalization" of childhood refers to a process by which organized arrangements, chiefly the school system, influence children's lives and organize their days. It requires individuation, formal membership, registration and timetables (Frones, 1994: 150). The educational system varies according to curriculum, age grading, nature of the system and teaching styles. Schools vary greatly in size, in their surroundings and in their ideology. The consequences of institutionalization can be discovered only through empirical analysis of the actual organization of a particular educational landscape.

Institutionalization is a secular trend, which has transformed childhood. It is a process to the seen in its doubleness: on the one side a protecting and caring process, on the other side a process which demonstrates a trend towards separating children's and adults' worlds. "Children's space of action is increasingly and qualitatively narrowed. The life world of children is more and more taken into protected rooms, sealed towards the natural world and limited towards other age-groups' action places" (Zinnecker, 1990: 142). Children are more and more acting as persons in their own right outside the family, first of all by way of an increasing "institutionalization", another dominant trend in our culture and often connected with individualization and individuation, but also with protection and marginalization.

Familialization

"Familialization" refers to the fusion of childhood into the family institution to such an extent that it defines an inseparable unit, which hampers the social visibility of its weaken part on its own. It thus penetrates children's lives as well as the way in which they are represented. Children's social identity is seen to minor that of their parents. The child is an open window to the family, and the family is portrayed in the child. The term informs us about children only implicitly, not as if they were autonomous actors, but rather as an extension of their natural milieu, the family (Barrett and McIntosh, 1982: 47).

An attempt to restore to childhood its social character has therefore to free the children from their "familialization", a process, which reduces them to their role within a parent-child relationship with all its connotations of emotional use-value, socialization, and invisibility within an essentially "private" institution (Oldman, 1994: 43). The process of "defamilialization" of the modern child is in which his/her relationship with adults is increasingly controlled by the employment conditions that the adult child workers negotiate with their employers. Children's propensity for sports, play, physical activity, mimicry and music are organized so as to provide remuneration for adults. Hengst (1987: 76) seeing the similarity in the employment conditions for child work with those for any other productive activity misleadingly refers to this as the "objective tendency" of the "liquidation of childhood".

In a pre-industrial era, servants were, to a large extent, children (Laslett, 1971: 89) and there were considerable transfers of child labour between households according to need. In industrial times, older girls (again, often not family members) did the bulk of childcare and domestic chores. The historical residue of this tradition that crept into this century lies in the notion of "mother's little helper" whereby children are "apprenticed" in a relatively non-serious way to their mother's domestic work.

There is an economic significance of childhood. Children create "child work", that is, work done by adults on the organization and control of child activities; "child work" is adult work but not work done by children ("children's work"). The term "child work" is used because of its theoretical closeness to "housework", and even "shift work", the evocative term used by some feminist writers to describe the low-status labour involved in the care and maintenance of others. In "child work", the child is the *object* of others' labour. "Child work" provides the means of subsistence for a significant proportion of the adult population. Only a small and decreasing proportion of this child work is done by parents on their own children and without financial reward.

Feminization

Children clearly belong to women's everyday lives, and are understood to do so to a much greater extent than to men's lives. Women are closely and unreflectively bound to children, and they have been repeatedly defined in terms of each other (Thorne, 1987: 95). Women and children are also often lumped together in a unity that is relegated – often through the fiction of "nature" – to the private sphere of families and households. Women undertake the main part of childcare, and they tend to develop the stronger emotional bonds with children.

Women more often than men have taken care of children, that children historically were always a "women's business" much more than a male responsibility, there are good reasons for holding the view that one should, may not speak in general terms about children's relationship with adult, but rather distinguish between women and men – or perhaps even better mothers and fathers.

The feminist theory[1] has not broken the inheritance of marginalizing children in discussing gender issues related to children. It has unfortunately remained just as functionalist and adult-centred as main/male stream social science. In its legitimate search for a "women's stand point", feminist studies have revolved mostly around how women and women's life worlds could be made visible in a research that so far was hegemonically dominated by a male perspective. Irrespective of possible shortcomings of feminist research, which it has in common with other adult research, it remains a fact that women are much more involved with children than are men. Children are thus not only much more together with women (although not always their mothers), they also more often have to share the well-known phenomenon of "feminization of poverty", which unfortunately might as well be called "pauperization of childhood".

NOTE

1. It means maternal power or mothers with regard to their children. Some feminist theorists have argued for a diversified conceptualization of power, seeing maternal power not simply as women's "power over" children, *i.e.* as domination, but as "power to", *i.e.* as power over another person that can be used for the benefit of that person.

3

Functioning of the Sample Schools

School is a special environment where a certain quality of life and certain type of activity and occupation are provided with the job of securing child's development on desirable lines. "The school as a social institution is a setting where crucially, adult authority is more salient as less challengeable than at home" (Mayall, 1994: 122). School differs from the home in its character as an institution with accepted social goals and norms formalized and implemented through the regime; or as has been neatly put: standardized modes of behaviour (Giddens, 1979: 96).

School problems are numerous. According to Kovaqik (1994: 113) the most criticized features of school education are: regimentation, lack of individualization; a rigid system of seating, grouping, grading and marking; and the authoritarian role of the teacher. The school has a low-grade recognition of children's physical health. The implications of compulsory all-day schooling as regards to health maintenance are a matter of serious concern. Some childrens are aware of health damaging aspect of school routines, boredom and tedium, noise, stressful social relations with adult and children, "from which and from whom they cannot escape" (Mayall, 1994: 123). Another major problem is the lack of strong interpersonal relationship between students and teachers. The students do not feel free to discuss their problems, *viz.* classroom teaching, course content and examinations, etc. with the teachers. The teachers also usually do not encourage the students to do so.

The quality of schooling is very low in most cases, with inadequate infrastructure, large class sizes, demoralized and under-trained teachers, uninspiring methods and overburdened curricula. A key determinant of demand for primary education is not so much the absence of schools but the fact that those, which do exist, do not function properly. In some cases schools have become the worst violators of children's rights, containing, suppressing, intimidating and silencing children.

School does not mean just education and school work. The most important factor for many children, at least for some time, is that school is first of all the place where peers are met, friendships are made, and some fun is experienced. It is a place to learn not just from adults but also from their own kind, people of their own age or only a little older. The distance to be overcome is not so wide; the models offered by examples of those who are just "a little bit older" are very often more powerful and appealing than those set by adults. School is not simply one aspect among others of a child's education, it was conceived from the start as the foremost, and ultimately the only one. Its time-tables occupy the child's whole day; its programmes encourage indirect knowledge to the detriment of experience even where practical training is concerned; its discipline defines the ideal behaviour, of a child in terms of passivity and blind obedience under an educational system of intimidation (Meyer, 1983: 11).

Educational administration is the dynamic side of education. Administration means management, control and arrangement. Every institution needs administration for its effective working. School is also an institution and its machinery needs efficient administration for smooth functioning. School is the "systematic arrangement for a definite purpose". School organization is a part organization, which refers to arrangement for providing efficient instructions to the pupils in the school. To maintain the efficiency of the educational system teachers are expected to co-operate with the administration. Administrative requirements mainly relate to teaching hours, time-schedules, time-tables, regularity of attendance, procedures to be observed for marking and assessing the performance of students, etc.

The principal or the administrative head holds the key position in a school. S/he is the co-coordinating agency, which keeps the balance and ensures the harmonious development of the whole institution. In our sample schools it is observed that the head has a sympathetic imagination in his/her dealings with the staff and students. None of the heads of the schools surveyed is ever seen to be an autocrat who simply issues commands which are to be carried out both by the staff and students on the good old principle: "They are not to reason why". A good quality marked in the principal or head in the sample schools it that they establish a friendly relationship with their pupils.

The procedure that uniquely identifies an individual is individuation. The process lays emphasis on individual rights, equality of opportunity and equality of outcome. This means an intervention in the life of an autonomous individual. The principle of individuation states that everyone has the democratic right to his/her own opinion. It gives new emphasis on children's formal rights and weakens the parents or household authority.

The central function of both schools and families is the nurture and education of children. Family has an overriding role in shaping personality and determining the well-being of the children. On the other hand a teacher is the centre of attraction for the students. A tactful and intelligent teacher can create an atmosphere of joyful reading for his learners in order to reap the product in heap. Education is a triangular process representing teacher and pupil as two arms and social environment at the base of the triangle. No school system can fruitfully perform without the co-operation of parents with teachers. Expecting co-operation from the parents, "parents-day" are also organized by the schools. In such meetings the teachers welcome suggestions from the parents and let the parents know the shortcomings in their children both in the academic sphere and in the extra-curricular activities of the school. If a relationship of confidence, friendliness and mutual support has not been previously established, a parent-teacher meeting can become a confrontation between adversaries rather than a dialogue held for the benefit of the child (Kaplan, 1971: 261). A school can bridge the distance between families and schools by surveying parents to find out their concerns and opinions about school.

While visiting the house of a respondent, his father violently retaliated to his resent unpleasant experience at the school and stated:

> "I am not pleased with the environment of the school. The unfriendly attitude of some of the teachers hurts me a lot. The Principal is also very strict and does not encourage parents to meet any teacher in the school excepting on parents' day."

The above report gives the picture of MCPS. It seems that some of the teachers are very harsh. For a good personality development of the child, both teachers and parents are responsible. The co-operation between the two will help the child grow up nicely. The statement of

Rakesh's father shows that he considers the existing practice as an unfair one.

A parent-teacher association can aid greatly in establishing co-operation between school and home. Only when the two come together and there is a perfect understanding between the parents and the teachers, then the educational development of the child can be understood in the correct perspective. Parent-teacher co-operation is based on a bi-lateral understanding of triangular relationship. The parties concerned are the parent, the teacher and the child. The understanding centres on the growing personality of the child. It is an association to which all the staff and as many of the parents as wish to may belong. By establishing a close contact with the parents of his pupils the teacher can gain the co-operation of the home and thus make his task easier. The teacher will understand the pupil better, and the parent will know better where care is needed. The chances of school and home pulling in different directions will be greatly reduced. It is always advisable to have students and parents represented on the board of management or governing body of a school. This ensures a greater interest being taken in the school by the students and parents.

Schools that have the lowest level of student achievement are also the most likely to describe a very low level of parent involvement. Very few parents talk with their children about education and provide day-to-day monitoring and support of schoolwork. Parents set and hold high expectations for their children. However, only a few parents help their children develop problem-solving skills. Many schools communicate to parents what their child is doing in school and what the teachers' expectations are. Thus, sometimes the parents and teachers share together regarding the future of the child.

A smooth functioning of the educational system and the satisfactory performance of the role of the school teacher require that teachers do not let interpersonal academic differences develop into feelings of inferiority or superiority. Policies are made at different levels. Where the social system provides for a dichotomy between policy making and teaching, policies are generally binding on the teachers. Education is so organized that the norms, standards and values that govern the system of education are consistent with those that the system tries to inculcate. Rosenholtz (1985: 199) maintains that collaborative activity in the school where the decision-making is shared by faculty members and the leader results in school success. The staff is instrumental in and instrumental to school effectiveness.

Hence, the members of the staff are seen to be adequately qualified and experienced. The staff includes administrative staff, instructional staff and non-teaching staff.

At secondary school level, teachers look upon themselves primarily as teachers, *i.e.* as persons who have made pedagogy their profession. They are concerned with the process of teaching. They claim expert knowledge in a field more than in any particular subject they may be called upon to teach. The major assumption on which the teacher-student relationship depends is that the teacher has knowledge which he wishes to impart to his pupils and that the latter desires to acquire it. This need not imply that knowledge is something like an entity, which is to be stored and dispensed with. Knowledge need not be considered as finite and to be acquired once for all. But even if it is to be viewed as a continual pursuit, the assumption in the educative process is that the teacher is ahead of his pupil in this pursuit and that he can effectively guide the pupil. There is, therefore, an element of distance and authority in the teacher-pupil relationship.

During the study, it is marked that many teachers maintain distance with their students. In the school hours they are seen either in the classroom taking class or in the staff common room. They do not interact with the students outside the classroom. Their relationship with the students is only confined to the teaching hours. It is further observed that when some students go to the staff common room for some clarification in their studies, the teachers reply them just in limited sentences without encouraging further discussion. Many students feel dissatisfied with such attitude of their teachers, which make them feel irritated. As result, many loose their interest in those subjects where they fail to clarity their doubts.

The role of a teacher cannot obviously be the same at all levels of education. And even at the same level of education, the role may be conceived differently in different systems of education. It is said that student nuisance is a common factor now-a-days. College students are addicted to it while school students are also not completely free of it. The mode of controlling student nuisance is different for different teachers. Though in our sample schools punishment is given to students for nuisance, still a cordial relationship exists between the teacher and the student.

It is significant to note a peculiar characteristic of many of the students studying in class IX and class X of CSBZS and MGHS. The students are mentally disgusted and have lost their interest in studies, as the concerned teachers do not teach their subjects properly. They feel the school atmosphere suffocated due to the threatening environment that prevails during the school hours. They have developed a fear complex in their minds due to the punishment pattern. They are sometimes severely punished for indiscipline in the school and also for not doing homework. All these things have physically and mentally overloaded them. As a result of this, some students have become escapists. They go home during the recess period and do not turn up in the second half due to fear of the teachers. This is mostly seen in both the Oriya medium schools.

The school is as formal agency of education offering two-way traffic to promote learning and teaching simultaneously. If writing makes a man perfect, which of course comes at a subsequent stage, reading makes a man exact. But the foundation of this must necessarily be laid down at the grassroots, *i.e.* from the stage of school libraries and then ultimately to public libraries. A library is an important organ of educational machinery. It is a rich spring from which knowledge flows out to irrigate the wide field of education and culture. In the words of Bacon, "Libraries are the shelves where all the relics of saints full of virtue and that without delusion and importance are preserved and reposed". With the explosion of knowledge and for the sake of widening of mental horizon, we cannot afford to remain contented in the narrow grooves of the textbooks. The thirst for knowledge has become insatiable, with the introduction of many new subjects in the modern school curriculum. The syllabus in each subject, insists on thorough study of not only textbooks but also wants supplementary reading of books as much as possible.

The four sample schools follow the colonial form of education, with inappropriate curricula and rigid and out-dated methods of teaching. All the schools function for six days in a week (Sunday being the holiday). The school day being approximately four to five hours at the primary level and five to seven hours for secondary school pupils. Each class has a class-teacher who is primarily responsible for the educational progress of the students. The class teacher normally takes the first class and s/he begins the class with a roll call. It is very disappointing to note in the sample schools that neither the students nor the teachers are aware of various provisions of the UN Convention on the Rights of the Child, 1989. The CRC serves as a tool of current international and national interests in redesigning knowledge on and with children.

The idea of rights with regard to children in matters of education is very new, and therefore many have not quite got used to the idea. Fifty years ago it would still have been unthinkable to challenge a decision made by a school headmaster concerning, for example, school expulsion, corporal punishment and examination results. Educational principles no longer have sovereign authority, but they have to stand the test of human decency and justice with regard to children. The relation between education and the rights of the child displays several aspects, each of which is far more comprehensive than would be expected. Education and children's rights have at least three major common grounds: First, the right to education; secondly, rights in education; finally, rights through education. These common grounds have already been established in several national and international rules. Establishing a respectable relationship with children is an extremely hard and fundamental process that only recently has penetrated into social consciousness. In this respect, Convention is a starting point.

As far as the school-going children are concerned, the school bears a great responsibility in this matter, as the school is a most appropriate channel through which this task can be fulfilled both logically and continuously. Fundamentally speaking, education will have to re-orientate towards adopting a basic attitude with regard to respect for children's rights. This concentration on the aspect of attitude will have to go hand in hand with a re-evaluation of curriculum planning, study materials, teacher training and, in fact, the full range of educational purposes, content and practices.

Taking into consideration that school concern the child directly, the school-going children should be given opportunities to comment on and to participate in the organization of education and school in general. What would be the point of setting up a complete theoretical educational process on the values of human rights, without putting it into practice as well? Failing to put it into practice would be sarcastic and disrespectful, not only towards adults, but especially towards the children. Dealing with these rights, means giving the child a place of genuine respect in disputes regarding explusion, disciplinary measures, the examination system, etc. All of this is directly connected with the demand for a clear set of rules that would give children at school a full legal position. There is no place, more suitable than school to show this respect.

St. Joseph's Convent High School

St. Joseph's Convent High School is a co-educational English Medium School. It is located in an isolated area on the outskirts of Sambalpur city. It was established in the year 1963 over an area measuring eight acres on the top of a small hill (Brooks hill) encompassed by a beautiful natural surrounding. This school was later affiliated to the ICSE Board in the year 1972 and has been following the prescribed pattern thereafter. The total students on roll of the school is 1558. Though the school has both primary and secondary sections the study has been confined to the students of the secondary level only.

The number of students with respect to their sex is shown in Table 3.1. The total number of teachers is 55 out of which 15 are

Table 3.1: Distribution of students of sample schools in terms of their educational standard and sex

Educational Standard	*Sex*	*Sample Schools*				*Total*
		SJCHS (ICSE)	*MCPS (CBSE)*	*CSBZS (HSC)*	*MGHS (HSC)*	
Class-VI	M	38	91	160	—	289
	F	22	87	—	116	225
Class-VII	M	32	67	174	—	273
	F	23	60	—	104	187
Class-VIII	M	34	65	287	—	386
	F	24	55	—	122	201
Class-IX	M	27	58	258	—	343
	F	21	61	—	153	235
Class-X	M	25	62	190	—	277
	F	20	47	—	53	120
Total		266	653	1069	548	2536

males and the remaining 40 are females. Of the 5 non-teaching staff, only one is a male and the remaining 4 are females. In addition to these there are 12 ministerial staff[1] , where the male-female ratio is 8:4 (Table 3.2). The result of class X during the last five years is depicted in Table 3.3.

Relatively more numbers of students from upper income bracket as compared to others are found in this school. The functioning hours of the school is between 7.45 am to 1.00 pm. The school starts functioning with a prayer (devotional song). On a normal day the students attend 8 classes with a short break of 20 minutes after the

Table 3.2: Distribution of staff members of sample schools in terms of their post and sex

Post held by staff members	*Sex*	*Sample Schools*				*Total*
		SJCHS (ICSE)	*MCPS (CBSE)*	*CSBZS (HSC)*	*MGHS (HSC)*	
Teaching	M	15	20	28	—	63
	F	40	33	07	15	95
Non-teaching	M	01	06	03	—	10
	F	04	—	—	01	05
Ministerial	M	08	06	04	03	21
	F	04	04	—	03	11
Total		72	69	42	22	205

Table 3.3: Results of Class-X in sample schools during last five years (1997-2001)

Year	*Result*	*Sample Schools*			
		SJCHS (ICSE)	*MCPS (CBSE)*	*CSBZS (HSC)*	*MGHS (HSC)*
1997	Appeared	52	80	246	60
	Passed	50	77	232	38
	Percentage	96 %	96 %	94 %	63 %
1998	Appeared	47	86	252	57
	Passed	43	83	208	23
	Percentage	91 %	96 %	82 %	40 %
1999	Appeared	51	99	218	58
	Passed	46	96	165	41
	Percentage	90 %	97 %	75 %	70 %
2000	Appeared	48	110	227	64
	Passed	45	103	153	47
	Percentage	94 %	93 %	67 %	73 %
2001	Appeared	46	105	178	56
	Passed	44	100	126	39
	Percentage	96 %	95 %	71 %	70 %

fourth period. The school uniform has an attractive combination of gray coloured pant and white shirt for boys. The colour remains the same for female students who wear gray coloured skirt and white blouse. Black shoes and white socks are common for all. The students put on this uniform throughout the week, except on Wednesday when they put on white uniform.

All the students take keen interest in various extra-curricular activities of the school like NCC[2], boy scout/girl guide, athletics, annual function, etc. The principal is strict with respect to the order and discipline inside the school campus. The classteacher has a regular practice of sending the progress report of the annual and terminal examination to the parents. All the parents of the students are requested to join together once in a year on the parents' day. This creates a scope for both the parents and the teachers to get closer and make some constructive and meaningful discussions for the betterment of the school as a whole and for the students in particular. No transportation facility is provided either to the staff or to the students, and therefore, they make their own arrangement for conveyance.

Madnabati Central Public School

Madnabati Central Public School is an English Medium School. It is situated at the outskirts of the city. The school follows the Central Board of Secondary Education (CBSE) course for educating its students. This syllabus is common for all the central schools in the country. This co-educational institution was established in the year 1980 over an area of 5.6 acres of land. Later on it got affiliated to the Central Board in the year 1983. The attendance registers of different classes show the total strength of the school to be 1873.

Table 3.1 gives a picture of the students studying in different classes (class VI to class X) with respect to sex ratio in classes. The total number of teaching staff, non-teaching staff and ministerial staff with respect to their sex is depicted in Table 3.2. The students taking class X Board examinations are found to have performed well for the last five years (1997–2001). The appeared and passed percentage is represented in Table 3.3.

The school functions between 9.45 am and 4.00 pm. The day starts with an assembly prayer in an open space inside the school campus. During a day the students attend nine periods with one short break and a relatively longer break. The colour of the school uniform makes the compound look beautiful. The boys wear navy blue coloured pant and white shirt, whereas the female students wear navy blue coloured skirt and white blouse. It is compulsory for all the students to put on the school badge and school belt. On Saturdays they participate in the drill wearing white uniform (Plate 1).

The school provides good library facility to the students. The school encourages the students to participate in various extra-curricular activities. The students also participate in the inter-school debate/essay competitions. The principal, staffs and students are punctual at school.

Plate 1: Students' Assembly

The school compound is neat and clean, looks colourful with a beautiful flower garden. The school invites all the parents to attend its annual day celebration. Examinations are conducted at regular intervals: annual examination, half-yearly examination and quarterly tests[3]. The results of all these examinations are sent to the parents so that they are aware of the progress of their children. The school maintains five numbers of buses. It solves the transportation problem of the students and the teachers coming from a relatively longer distance. In one corner of the school premises, there lies a cycle-stand for the convenience of students and staff coming by cycle.

Chandra Sekhar Behera Zilla School

Chandra Sekhar Behera Zilla School is a Boys' High School. It is an Oriya medium school located at the heart of the city close to a junction where the roads are always busy. The syllabus of the school is affiliated to the High School Certificate Examination (HSC) course. It is one of the oldest schools in the city established in the year 1954. The school was taken over by the Government in the year 1957.The school extends over an area of 6.519 acres of land.

The number of students in different classes is presented in Table 3.1. The total number of students in this school is 1069. Most of the teachers in the school are males; although a handful of female teachers also work here. All the 3 members of the non-teaching staff and 4 ministerial staff are males (Table 3.2). The school report shows a satisfactory performance of the students in class X (Table 3.3).

The course structure of HSC Board is easier as compared with other courses. The school starts with a time of devotional prayer at 11.15 am. The last period ends at 4.30 pm. The students attend 7 periods in a day. After the fourth period there is a recess, where the students find time for recreation and taking their tiffin. Some of the students also go home to have some food during the break. A few others buy food items from *thela* (mobile stalls) just outside the entrance gate of the school.

The school uniform remains the same all through the week. Putting on shoes and socks is not compulsory. The distinguished colour combination of the uniform, that is, navy blue coloured pant and white shirt increases the beauty of the school. Among all extra-curricular activities in the school, the NCC is given more importance. Almost all the senior boys are given this training. The school has an ill-managed library with no up-to-date books. The school also lacks the improved teaching aids. The subjective nature[4] of questions in all the examinations has led to the poor performance of the students.

The headmaster is a lenient man. Some senior teachers are very strict for which discipline is maintained within the school premises. In this school there is hardly any meaningful interaction between parents and teachers. Quarters are allotted only to a few senior teachers (including headmaster) within the school compound. The school does not provide any transport facilities to neither the staffs nor the students.

Municipal Girls' High School

Municipal Girls' High School is an Oriya medium school, situated in a crowded area at the centre of the city. The school is governed by the Sambalpur Municipality Corporation. The students follow the High School Certificate Examination (HSC) course. The school was established over a small area of 1.5 acres of land; in the year 1964. It got soon its recognition from the Board in the following year (1965). The school has teaching facilities for girl students studying between class VI and class X. The total strength of the school is 548.

The distribution of the students in different classes is shown in Table 3.1. The following table shows the total number of teaching and non-teaching staff in the school. Records show that the results of this school in the previous year were not as good as that of the other sample schools. The performance of the students in class X is presented in Table 3.3.

It is seen that relatively higher percentage of girls of lower income bracket are studying in this school as it is less expensive compared to other sample schools. All though the week (excepting Saturday) the school starts its day at 10.30 am and ends at 4.00 pm. On Saturday the school timing deviates and morning classes are held between 6.45 am and 11.00 am. Before the students go to their respective classrooms, all the teachers and the students assemble together for a prayer. A student attends as many as seven classes in a day excepting Saturday.

The descent royal blue coloured skirt and white blouse brings a sober look on the face of the students. The *Ganesh puja*[5] and *Saraswati puja*[6] are celebrated in the school by the students. The school provides facility for indoor games like carom, chess, ludo, etc. and outdoor games like badminton, basketball, etc. The school has a game teacher and big playground.

The compound of the school is very neat and clean. The beautiful flowers and croton leaves add to the beauty of the campus. Most of the students come to school by foot and only a few come by bicycle. Though all the parents are requested to attend the annual function and the *pujas* in the school, yet only a few of them turn up. This shows that the parents are less associated and less involved with the teachers and the administration of the school. The progress reports of the students in the school examinations are not being regularly sent to the parents.

NOTES

1. It includes all the peons, sweepers, gardeners and watchmen.
2. NCC (National Cadet Corps) is a training given to the students for their physical fitness. The trained up students march on the parade ground during Independence Day and Republic Day.
3. Quarterly tests means examinations conducted in the interval of every three months.
4. By subjective nature of the question, I mean long or essay type questions.
5. This worship is performed on the fourth day in the month of *Bhadra* (August-September) for obtaining blessings of Lord Ganesh for the enhancement of wisdom and knowledge.
6. This *puja* is offered in honour of Goddess Saraswati for acquiring knowledge. This is done on the fifth day in the month of *Magha* (January–February). Mostly the students to attain success in studies perform this *puja*.

4

Course Curriculum

In a school, teachings go as per the course curriculum throughout the academic year. The student is thereby exposed to new ideas and new subjects. The classroom teaching to the child goes through a process of digestion and finally, assumes a process of reproduction in annual examination. Everything just strictly moves through a demarcated grove called "curriculum". Basically curriculum in its full sense comprises all the opportunities for learning provided by a school or institution. The lexicographical meaning of curriculum is a course to be run for reaching a certain goal. The term curriculum has been used in a variety of ways to designate a programme for a given subject matter at the specific grade level.

There is a tendency in all the sample schools to crowd the syllabus of each subject with too many facts that are of little significance in children's lives. The curriculum makers at the school level are more concerned with logical and scientific demands of the subjects than the needs, the psychology and the interests of the learners. The sample students are exposed to too extensive textbooks, excessively complex subject matter, unintelligible formulations, a host of scientific terms, abstract concepts, encyclopaedic facts in textbooks, etc. The mass of teaching material is disproportionate to the age of the student; the degree of difficulty of textbooks rises irregularly and disproportionately; the potential didactic effectiveness is slight (Kovaqik, 1994: 112). It appears as if the workload of the school children is sometimes greater than that of the adults.

The increasing pace of advancement in knowledge demands an increasing rate of change in educational system, *viz.* curriculum content, teaching and learning method and the teacher and student attitudes. These changes make the teacher more closely associated with curriculum makers because they are the people who possess the appropriate professional training and put the curriculum into practice.

Patton and Mercer (1996: 110) discuss that the more time the teachers devote to centres; the better the children take advantage of centres' unique learning environments. The present curriculum does not mean only the academic subjects but also includes the totality of experience that a pupil receives through the manifold activities that go on in the school, in classroom, library, laboratory, playground, etc.

The curriculum is made such that it accounts not only for work but also for leisure. The items in the curriculum are interrelated and related to life. Bredekamp and Copple (1997: 137) explain that the skills and concepts are taught through observations of teachers and children, laboratory experiences with children, small-group interactions, videotapes, reading and discussions of pre-professionals own experiences with children. The present curriculum is dominated by the examinations. The types of questions asked in the examination determine the importance of the contents and the weightage given to the topics of study. The examinations are a powerful force in determining what is learned and what is taught. They influence students' method of study and students' attitude towards education. They also influence the faculties' method of teaching. The syllabus of every course is based on the objectives of the subject. Assessment cannot be accurately done unless it is known what is to be assessed. Schools are not only concerned with knowledge transmission; they reproduce and mediate social division of labour. Schools are thus engaged in the distribution and allocation of degrees whose value is socially exchanged for.

When one sits down and analyzes, the realization dawns that our children are actually going nowhere. They are only undergoing a system of learning by rote and that would definitely not take them too far. Says Ranjan Acharya, Vice President, Human Resource Development, Wipro Ltd., "What is tomorrow going to be? It is going to be an age where problem solving, leadership, team management and working within teams will be the order of the day. We in India believe in cramming the children with whatever we can, not realizing whether the child is capable of assimilating it or not and then years later, at the age of 20 or so, start conducting workshops for them on leadership and self confidence etc. Does it make sense?" He says that it is important to instil all these qualities in children when they are young enough as habits begin early, especially thinking habits. He further adds that, "a child needs to learn, not cram a lesson. A child should have the zest and enthusiasm to learn. Children have this zest in them, but with our present educational system, we kill that zest slowly and permanently."

In the period from age 12 to 16, which in the majority of countries corresponds to Secondary Education, adolescents continue to need a formal education. It is a transitional stage in which the individual is no longer a child, but is not yet part of the adult world; it is a type of "moratorium"[1]. Neither can we forget that this is a period of important biological changes that occur in a relatively short space of time, and that these changes bring with them the need for the adolescent to construct a new identity as a subject. This leads, in turn, to the onset of psychological changes that the school respects and understands. Precisely in order to construct this new identity, adolescents need greater autonomy and need to be given increasing responsibility.

The revised curriculum has made the entire course structure vast. As Margarett Mead (1930: 322) has indicated: "We must direct our educational efforts to preparing children for coping effectively with the choices and changes which are confronting them." We are merely designing a "changing curriculum" rather than making a curriculum of change. Our sample students find it difficult to comprehend the new subject matters. For this they loose their interest in the classroom proceedings. The textbooks have also increased its volumetric size. This is an extra-burden to the school students in carrying a heavy load to the school daily. A female student of class VI, MCPC comments:

> "I stay at a distance of 3 kms from the school. I daily go to school on foot, carrying a heavy school bag having a load of thick textbooks and notebooks of eight periods. I feel very tired after returning from school."

The statement of Shrabani speaks not only of the heavy weight she carries on her back but also the heaviness of her mind. She carries the heavy load all along her back to the school daily. This makes her school life monotonous and certainly takes away the fun and pleasure of school life. If the books are heavy, life becomes still more difficult.

Feldek's poem in defense of children (1988: 6) describing school children as slaves carrying burdens physical and psychological is no exaggeration in this respect. The very weight of textbooks children have to carry with them to school often exceeds the limit set by the Ministry of Education. Outdoor physical exercises in school, which would contribute to physical and mental regeneration, are seriously lacking.

It is observed that the students of the sample schools carry a heavy load of school bag at their back while going to school. The thick textbooks and notebooks of all the periods, along with a tiffin-box not only increase the volume but also the weight of the school bag. It is also noticed that in addition to the heavy school bag, the sample students are seen carrying the different tasks assigned to them in the project works. The English medium school students have the project work in almost all subjects. It becomes quite inconvenient and difficult for the students who live at far off places from the school. It also becomes hard for them who go to school on foot or by cycle. This clearly reflects that the revised course structure overloads the students and the weight of the heavy school bag also becomes an extra burden for them (Case Study 1).

The hardship starts right at home when straight from bed the child is pulled out and got ready for school even before his faculties are awaken. S/he is groomed and stuffed into a uniform and packed off with a loaded bag on the back. School bag has become an inevitable burden for the child. It is observed that an average child carries, strapped to his back like a pack-mule not less than 6–8 kgs of books, note-books and other paraphernalia of modern education in addition to it a lunch-box and water bottle. Some children on account of this daily burden develop a stoop and hang their arms forward like a chimpanzee while walking and also there are a few cases of spinal injuries in the children.

One major drawback in all our sample schools is the lack of teaching aids. The inclusion of project works in the course has increased the burden of the students. Collecting information, picture cuttings and taking photographs consume much of their time. Most of their parents are found engaged in helping them. This is also a matter of expense. The observation of the study reveals that the quality of teaching has a greater impact on the students. It is seen that in our sample schools some of the teachers are untrained. This creates a big gap between the students and the teachers. The teachers are unable to meet the exact requirements of the students in a classroom.

During the course of my study I happened to attend the teaching in MCPS of class IX. It was significant to note that, though the teacher had vast knowledge on the subject he could not express his thoughts. He used very high-sounding words, lengthy sentences with ornamental languages, which went beyond the understanding of the students. This creates a state of confusion in their minds. The level of teaching in the classroom is also an important criterion for consideration. This unnecessarily becomes taxation for the school children.

As things stand today, the teacher occupies the centre of the stage in the grand opera of learning. Some of our sample teachers do not understand the dynamics of communication in the classroom and have too simplistic a model of the classroom in mind. The teacher is like a river and all students are like small canals drawing water from it. Some canals draw more water than others, as some bright boys and girls in the classroom learn more from the teacher than some others who are not so bright. When a teacher teaches in the classroom in an abstract level, it becomes difficult for the average students and obviously boring for the dull students to understand the teaching. In our sample schools, it is noticed that some of the teachers are unable to reach every student in the classroom because they themselves are untrained. But in some cases it is seen that the teacher's level of teaching is very high that it surpasses the understanding of most of the students in the classroom. These reasons create a wider gap between the teacher and students which results to be a burden for the school children (Plate 2).

Plate 2: Teacher Imparting Teaching

Good teaching lies in the ability to reach students and motivate them to learn, regardless of their background or ability and good teachers are for the most part, born, not made. It is the teacher who is the key to good teaching. What we read and hear, we forget but what we do, we understand. Good teachers use this principle to incorporate activities, demonstrations and role-playing in their classrooms. They encourage students to really get excited about creative writing.

There has been inclusion of many diversified courses of study into the syllabus, for which the teachers are orientated to the revised curricula through in-service education. The traditional curriculum was narrowly conceived, unpsychologically planned and ineffectively executed. The present course structure is an accelerated and enriched curriculum. This challenging curriculum engages the students in school by drawing clear connections between learning and the world beyond school. It is marked in the sample schools that there has been lot of changes in the course structure within the last ten years. In addition to this the quality of teaching in the schools has also changed.

While interviewing a teacher of SJCHS, she stated:

> "I find it difficult to take classes as I am not acquainted with the new course structure. No refresher course or any training is given to us to add to our understanding new concepts and theories. What I had read during graduation level is now taught in class X."

The aforesaid statement reveals the inconvenience the teacher faces due to the upgradation of the course curriculum. It is difficult for the teacher to understand and explain the students what they themselves have not understood. It appears that training camps are essential for the teachers, so that they gain some knowledge about the modern concepts and theories. The inability of the teachers to handle a course turns out to be a great problem for the students.

Integrating curriculum requires complex change, which may make teachers, school administrators and parents uncomfortable. Hargreaves, Earl, Moore and Manning (2001: 83) point out that integrated or inter-disciplinary curriculum is one of the most ambitious yet also contentious aspects of educational reform, as it seeks to connect classroom learning to the lives and understandings of all students.

A careful observation reveals that the ICSE course pattern has taken a new shape as compared to twelve years before. There has been inclusion of project works[2] in eight subjects. There was no computer provision in the school about seven years ago. However, now the students of the primary section also operate computer. Computer teaching is given to all the students from class IV. In addition to the Orissan History, the students are now taught Indian History as well as World History. The school students find it very tough to grasp the difficult practical papers in Physics, Chemistry and Biology. Ten years ago these experiments were being done by college-going students at the graduation level. Many parents are unable to help their children particularly in the science subjects (Plate 3).

Plate 3: Students Doing Chemistry Practical

Similar problems are also faced by the students studying the CBSE course. Many teachers feel that they are incapable of handling the revised course. They do not feel confident to take practical classes in different subjects. As a result, many chapters remain uncovered. For instance, the Geography paper has changed quite a lot. The students have to get themselves acquainted with maps of Orissa, India and World. They are not only to fill up the blank outline maps with places in different locations but also to know the roadways and railway routes. The present course contents of Economics taught to the students of class VIII and class IX were taught to students at the Intermediate level five years ago.

The students following the HSC course are not even exception to this. The syllabus of science paper has become vast. Earlier it was only a single subject but now it is sub-divided into three different papers: Physics, Chemistry and Biology. The students show poor performance in the examinations due to lack of proper infrastructure facilities for the practical papers. It is difficult for the Oriya medium students to grasp the English subject. Earlier this paper was comparatively easier, but now there has been inclusion of poetry and drama. Precise writing and comprehension are also included in the language paper. Therefore, now many students get disinterested in this subject, as they find it very tough (Plate 4).

Plate 4: Students Working on Computers

It is quite significant to observe the picture of our sample classrooms. The very physical structure of the classroom speaks the relationship between the teacher and the taught. The rows of students, all facing the teacher (anu not one another), and the teacher on a head-table, physically depicts the classroom paradigm. In some cases it is observed that the teachers even get raised platforms to talk down to. The teacher pronounces loudly and clearly that the students are empty (ignorant), invert (incapable of active search and discovery), and the teachers are full (knowledgeable), and all that is required is for the teacher to let the knowledge flow out towards the ignorant students.

In such a typical classroom situation children are mostly required to keep quite and listen to the teacher. They are required to reproduce given information on demand. They are not required to ask questions, in fact, they are severely dissuaded from indulging in the subversive activity of asking questions, especially of the fundamental type. It is noticed that question asking is not a behaviour that teachers seek to promote. Though officially not banned, in practice the teachers use an array of techniques to discourage it. "Don't you know even this?", "Were you sleeping?", "Don't ask silly questions",—are some of the not so subtle pedagogic strategies to discourage question asking. There is yet another effective strategy noted that is to announce in the beginning of the class that questions can be asked only in the last 5 to 10 minutes. Of course, when the last five minutes arrive, there are so much left to be covered that the question session is postponed to another never-to-come time.

The following is a statement given by a male student of CSBZS studying in class IX:

> "I am not interested in reading Physics. My teacher does not allow me to ask questions for clarifying my doubts in the classroom. This makes me feel bad and sad."

The aforesaid statement reveals that Rohan does not like the atmosphere of his classroom. It appears that the Physics teacher does not give him much scope to clarify his doubts. This may adversely affect his performance. His comment further reflects that his teacher teaches mechanically and leaves the classroom even without asking the students whether they have understood the lesson or not. This is how the teacher makes the students feel dull in the classroom.

In our study the sample students responses to the subject that they feel most difficult have been analyzed. Of the 240 sample students, 56 (23.33%) feel Mathematics to be the most difficult subject followed by 54 (22.50%) students who find science to be the most difficult one. However, 49 (20.42%) sample students find English to be the most difficult subject whereas 47 (19.58%) students report History as the most difficult subject. 26 (10.83%) are of the opinion that Geography is most difficult paper and the remaining 8 (3.33%) students feel MIL[3] (Oriya/Hindi) to be the most difficult subject (Table 4.1a,b,c).

Table 4.1a: Distribution of sample students in terms of their sex and choice of most difficult subject [N=240]

Most Difficult Subject	*Sex*		*Total*
	Male	*Female*	
Mathematics	(42.86%) 24 (20%)	(57.14%) 32 (26.67%)	(100%) 56 (23.33%)
Science	(53.7%) 29 (24.17%)	(46.3%) 25 (20.83%)	(100%) 54 (22.5%)
English	(46.94%) 23 (19.17%)	(53.06%) 26 (21.67%)	(100%) 49 (20.42%)
History	(55.32%) 26 (21.67%)	(44.68%) 21 (17.5%)	(100%) 47 (19.58%)
Geography	(65.38%) 17 (14.17%)	(34.62%) 09 (7.5%)	(100%) 26 (10.83%)
MIL (Oriya/Hindi)	(12.5%) 01 (0.83%)	(87.5%) 07 (5.83%)	(100%) 08 (3.33%)
Total	(50%) 120 (100%)	(50%) 120 (100%)	(100%) 240 (100%)

The view of one of the teachers of MGHS is given below:

> "Some of the students show very poor performance in the examinations, as they find the subject too difficult. They do not get support in study matters from any family member at home. It is not only the duty of the teachers to help the students but it is equally the responsibility of the parents to provide all possible help to the children in their studies."

The above statement focuses on the feelings of the teacher for the parents. It appears as if the parents are blamed for the poor performance of the students. The poor educational background of the parents is one of the reasons for which the students do not get proper guidance from them. Most of the respondents of MGHS hail from a lower income bracket. Their parents find it difficult to send their children for coaching classes due to financial constraint. This situation creates a sort of inferiority complex in the minds of the students.

Table 4.1b: Distribution of sample students in terms of their course affiliation and choice of most difficult subject [N=240]

Most Difficult Subject	*Course Affiliation*			*Total*
	ICSE	*CBSE*	*HSC*	
Mathematics	(14.29%) 08 (10%)	(37.5%) 21 (26.25%)	(48.21%) 27 (33.75%)	(100%) 56 (23.33%)
Science	(40.74%) 22 (27.5%)	(40.74%) 22 (27.5%)	(18.52%) 10 (12.5%)	(100%) 54 (22.5%)
English	(38.78%) 19 (23.75%)	(26.53%) 13 (16.25%)	(34.69%) 17 (21.25%)	(100%) 49 (20.42%)
History	(40.43%) 19 (23.75%)	(25.53%) 12 (15%)	(34.04%) 16 (20%)	(100%) 47 (19.58%)
Geography	(30.77%) 08 (10%)	(38.46%) 10 (12.5%)	(30.77%) 08 (10%)	(100%) 26 (10.83%)
MIL (Oriya/Hindi)	(50%) 04 (5%)	(25%) 02 (2.5%)	(25%) 02 (2.5%)	(100%) 08 (3.34%)
Total	(33.33%) 80 (100%)	(33.33%) 80 (100%)	(33.34%) 80 (100%)	(100%) 240 (100%)

The opinions of our sample students relating to their difficulty in comprehending the subjects are also recorded. Table 4.2a,b reflects the difficulties a student confronts in dealing with these subjects. 70 (29.17%) sample students state that they face difficulty in certain subjects as they primarily feel the course to be vast in the concerned subjects. 64 (26.67%) of the sample students report the prime reason of facing difficulty is that the concerned teacher does not teach properly whereas for 54 (22.50%) students their disinterest in certain subjects is the main reason for finding the concerned subjects difficult. The subject itself seems to be tough for 52 (21.67%) sample students and that is their prime reason of difficulty. It can be concluded from the above analysis that a higher percentage of the sample students feel that the vastness of the course is the main reason for experiencing difficulty. One of the female students of MGHS studying in class VIII states:

Table 4.1c: Distribution of sample students in terms of their educational standard and choice of most difficult subject [N=240]

Most Difficult Subject	*Educational Standard*		*Total*
	ME (Class VI & VII)	*High Sch.(Class VIII to X)*	
Mathematics	(37.5%) 21 (14.58%)	(62.5%) 35 (36.46%)	(100%) 56 (23.33%)
Science	(59.26%) 32 (22.22%)	(40.74%) 22 (22.92%)	(100%) 54 (22.5%)
English	(55.1%) 27 (18.75%)	(44.9%) 22 (22.92%)	(100%) 49 (20.42%)
History	(93.62%) 44 (30.55%)	(6.38%) 03 (3.12%)	(100%) 47 (19.58%)
Geography	(57.69%) 15 (10.43%)	(42.31%) 11 (11.46%)	(100%) 26 (10.83%)
MIL (Oriya/Hindi)	(62.5%) 05 (3.47%)	(37.5%) 03 (3.12%)	(100%) 08 (3.33%)
Total	(60%) 144 (100%)	(40%) 96 (100%)	(100%) 240 (100%)

"The course structure seems to be quite vast so I-was unable to complete it. Some of the portions could not be covered before the examination. That led to my poor performance in the previous examination."

The statement of Roopali shows the reason of her poor performance in the previous examination. She feels that her poor performance in the examination is due to her inability to cover the vast course in time. That certainly caused frustration and tension for Roopali.

The sample students have different views regarding the course structure of their school. The Board of School Education has introduced advanced curriculum in almost all subjects in the schools. The inclusion of many new scientific concepts and theories has brought

Table 4.2a: Distribution of sample students in terms of their course affiliation and prime reason of facing difficulty in the concerned subject [N=240]

Reason of facing Difficulty	*Course Affiliation*			*Total*
	ICSE	*CBSE*	*HSC*	
Vast Course	(41.43%) 29 (36.25%)	(21.43%) 15 (18.75%)	(37.14%) 26 (32.5%)	(100%) 70 (29.17%)
Teacher does not teach well	(15.62%) 10 (12.5%)	(40.63%) 26 (32.5%)	(43.75%) 28 (35%)	(100%) 64 (26.67%)
Dis-interest in the subject	(50%) 27 (33.75%)	(40.74%) 22 (27.5%)	(9.26%) 05 (6.25%)	(100%) 54 (22.5%)
Subject is tough	(26.92%) 14 (17.5%)	(32.69%) 17 (21.25%)	(40.39%) 21 (26.25%)	(100%) 52 (21.66%)
Total	(33.33%) 80 (100%)	(33.33%) 80 (100%)	(33.34%) 80 (100%)	(100%) 240 (100%)

Table 4.2b: Distribution of sample students in terms of their educational standard and prime reason of facing difficulty in the concerned subject [N=240]

Reason of facing Difficulty	*Educational Standard*		*Total*
	ME (Class VI & VII)	*High Sch.(Class VIII to X)*	
Vast Course	(45.71%) 32 (22.22%)	(54.29%) 38 (39.58%)	(100%) 70 (29.17%)
Teacher does not teach well	(56.25%) 36 (25%)	(43.75%) 28 (29.17%)	(100%) 64 (26.67%)
Dis-interest in the subject	(79.63%) 43 (29.86%)	(20.37%) 11 (11.46%)	(100%) 54 (22.5%)
Subject is tough	(63.46%) 33 (22.92%)	(36.54%) 19 (19.79%)	(100%) 52 (21.66%)
Total	(60%) 144 (100%)	(40%) 96 (100%)	(100%) 240 (100%)

about mounting pressure on the children. As a result majority of the sample students feel that the course structure is too heavy. Our analysis proves that of the 240 sample students, only 59 (24.58%) find the course structure to be light; 87 (36.25%) opine that the syllabus is moderate in terms of difficulty level and the remaining 94 (39.17%) find it to be heavy (Table 4.3a,b). The inclusion of many newpapers

Table 4.3a: Distribution of sample students in terms of their opinion on course structure and course affiliation [N=240]

Course Affiliation	*Opinion on Course Structure*			*Total*
	Heavy	*Moderate*	*Light*	
ICSE	(45%) 36 (38.3%)	(32.5%) 26 (29.89%)	(22.5%) 18 (30.51%)	(100%) 80 (33.33%)
CBSE	(50%) 40 (42.55%)	(26.25%) 21 (24.13%)	(23.75%) 19 (32.2%)	(100%) 80 (33.33%)
HSC	(22.5%) 18 (19.15%)	(50%) 40 (45.98%)	(27.5%) 22 (37.29%)	(100%) 80 (33.34%)
Total	(39.17%) 94 (100%)	(36.25%) 87 (100%)	(24.58%) 59 (100%)	(100%) 240 (100%)

Table 4.3b: Distribution of sample students in terms of their opinion on course structure and educational standard [N=240]

Educational Standard	*Opinion on Course Structure*			*Total*
	Heavy	*Moderate*	*Light*	
ME (Class-VI & VII)	(48.61%) 70 (74.47%)	(31.25%) 45 (51.72%)	(20.14%) 29 (49.15%)	(100%) 144 (60%)
High School (Class-VIII to Class-X)	(25%) 24 (25.53%)	(43.75%) 42 (48.28%)	(31.25%) 30 (50.85%)	(100%) 96 (40%)
Total	(39.17%) 94 (100%)	(36.25%) 87 (100%)	(24.58%) 59 (100%)	(100%) 240 (100%)

and the modification of the course curriculum have made the subject matter quite complicated. The increasing level of difficulty in the syllabus is disproportionate to the age of the students and therefore many times remain beyond the comprehension level of the students. Further the heavy course structure makes the students feel strenuous and exhausted.

It is common knowledge that today's curriculum is only focused on transferring large amounts of information to the children while the focus should be on basic concepts and giving skills to the child on how to 'learn'. Currently, the Wipro programme tries to ensure that the process of learning becomes enjoyable for the child within the set boundaries of the examination boards. With time, Wipro is even looking at changing the syllabus of the Boards by demonstrating to them the effectiveness of their programme. Wipro is not only targeting the teachers and principals on becoming catalytic agents in their process of change, but are also putting in their efforts to communicate with as many parents as they can, in order to convince them on how important it is to educate the child the right way. For the overworked children of today, there sure is a ray of hope. What is the programme? Wipro—Applying thought in schools has been designed, keeping in mind the already busy schedule of teachers, the overbearing parents, the strenuous educational system and the young victims—the present day students.

The vast syllabus of the school has puzzled the minds of the students. Their daily schedule remains busy that they hardly get time for relaxation. Once I heard to hear the conversation of some students during the recess. Their talk shows that even during break they do not feel relaxed. Even there they are discussing about homework, tuitions, examinations and revision of the course. Both the school task and tuition homework become so heavy, that sometimes some students are seen doing the homework at school during recess. Some others are seen preparing for the tuition examinations. Thus the ever-increasing burden slowly but surely takes away the childhood from the school-going children (Chart 7).

Chart 7: Distribution of sample students in terms of their opinion on course structure [N=240]

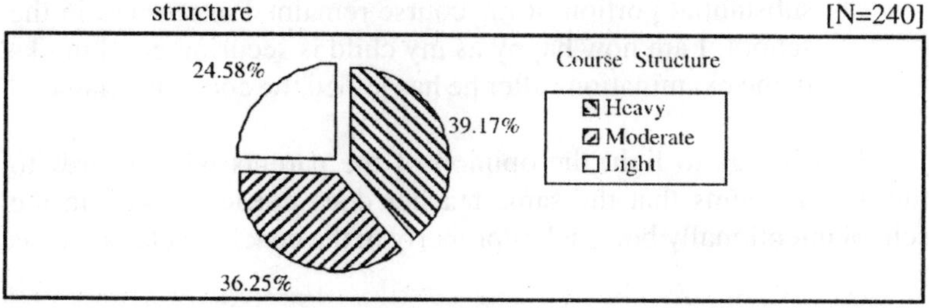

Education in the modern world is no longer a static affair. It expects the teachers to keep in touch with the latest trends in education. A teacher has to keep pace with the modern scientific life and its exacting demands. He has to reckon the increased alertness in modern pupils, their inquisitiveness and their shrewdness. Therefore a teacher has to recondition himself through in-service education in order to cope with every new situation, academic or disciplinary. In our sample schools, many teachers are not orientated to the revised curriculum. They are not clear about the theories and concepts of many new topics, for which they fail to meet the requirements of the students. The parents expect that their children should excel in academics. This prompts the parents to send their children for private coaching. Our study clearly shows that out of 240 sample students, 174 (72.50%) students attend coaching classes whereas only 66 (27.50%) stay away from it (Table 4.4a,b,c).

Table 4.4a: Distribution of sample students in terms of availing of tuition and sex

[N=240]

Sex	*Availing of Tuition*		*Total*
	Yes	*No*	
Male	(80%) 96 (55.17%)	(20%) 24 (36.36%)	(100%) 120 (50%)
Female	(65%) 78 (44.83%)	(35%) 42 (63.64%)	(100%) 120 (50%)
Total	(72.5%) 174 (100%)	(27.5%) 66 (100%)	(100%) 240 (100%)

The father of one of my respondents narrates:

> "I was forced to send my child to coaching classes, because substantial portion of the course remained uncovered in the school. I am now happy as my child is securing good marks in the examinations after he has joined the coaching classes."

This brings to light the opinion of the parents with regards to tuitions. It seems that the same teacher does not teach well in the school intentionally but teaches properly in the coaching classes so as

Table 4.4b: Distribution of sample students in terms of availing of tuition and age group [N=240]

Age Group	*Availing of Tuition*		*Total*
	Yes	*No*	
< 12 Yrs.	(41.67%) 30 (17.24%)	(58.33%) 42 (63.64%)	(100%) 72 (30%)
13-14 Yrs	(84.78%) 78 (44.83%)	(15.22%) 14 (21.21%)	(100%) 92 (38.33%)
> 15 Yrs.	(86.84%) 66 (37.93%)	(13.16%) 10 (15.15%)	(100%) 76 (31.17%)
Total	(72.5%) 174 (100%)	(27.5%) 66 (100%)	(100%) 240 (100%)

Table 4.4c : Distribution of sample students in terms of availing of tuition and course affiliation [N=240]

Course Affiliation	*Availing of Tuition*		*Total*
	Yes	*No*	
ICSE	(83.75%) 67 (38.51%)	(16.25%) 13 (19.7%)	(100%) 80 (33.33%)
CBSE	(70%) 56 (32.18%)	(30%) 24 (36.36%)	(100%) 80 (33.33%)
HSC	(63.75%) 51 (29.31%)	(36.25%) 29 (43.94%)	(100%) 80 (33.34%)
Total	(72.5%) 174 (100%)	(27.5%) 66 (100%)	(100%) 240 (100%)

to attract the students. The students' performance is better in the school because the teacher must be revising the course thoroughly in the tuition classes. This becomes a burden for the students to attend one or more tuition. Similarly it is an extra burden for the parents for spending money both for school and tuition.

I have spoken to many parents who feel the need to get extra tutoring or special classes for average or even above average children. Their comment is that many children do not know the basic or they cannot understand things that are too abstract. It is a sad state when average children are not getting the education they need in regular classes and parents are paying money for them to learn in a way they should have been learning in the first place. Good teachers accommodate students who have difficulty and challenge those who need the challenge. Unless we have more good teachers we will enter into a two-tiered system where those who can afford special help will pay for it and those who cannot, will suffer.

It is noteworthy to observe that some students go for two to three tuitions in a day. It must be monotonous on the part of a school student to attend more than two tuitions in a day after spending long six hours in the school. The difficult course structure and the attitude of teachers towards classroom teaching force the students to attend tuitions almost in all subjects. As a matter of tactics many teachers do not teach the subjects assigned to them properly in school. As a result the students find it difficult to comprehend the subject properly. This forces them to join coaching classes. It is interesting to note that contrary to the classroom teaching, the same teacher teaches the subject to the satisfaction of the students in the coaching classes.

Similar situation is found in all the sample schools. The students are mostly seen taking tuitions in Mathematics, Physics, Chemistry and English. In lower classes it is observed that the tutor generally comes to the house of the students. But in class IX and class X mostly the students go to the tutor's house. A student takes tuition of each subject three days in a week. But during examinations the tutor teaches his subjects four days in a week. It is also seen that the same teacher intentionally does not teach well in the school but teaches very nicely in the coaching classes so as to attract the students. In the tuition classes the teacher discusses many model test papers and conducts examinations. In this context a student has to do simultaneously his school homework and tuition task. In fact, that becomes very difficult for a school student. What is recorded below is a statement of a female student of class X, studying in MPCS:

> "I attend three tuition classes in some days, one tuition before going to school and two in the evening after returning from school. I hardly get time to complete my school homework for which I very often get scolded by my teacher."

The above statement given by Sunita clearly indicates that she remains busy throughout the day. It seems that a major part of her time gets consumed by attending coaching classes. As a result she does not find enough time to do her school home task. This puts enormous pressure on her leading to a stressful life. Her teacher is displeased for her negligence in performing her home task. This gradually makes her mentally upset and aggressive.

It is observed that in majority of the cases the students go to the tutor's house and in a few cases the tutor comes to the houses of the students. Attending school and then going to different tutors' houses in a single day is quite tiring for the students. Another factor that makes them feel tired is the distance of the tutor's house and the mode of conveyance. It is also inconvenient and insecure for the students of lower age group to go to tutor's house alone. Analysis of the data reveals that, out of 174 sample students, 98 (56.32%) go to the tutors' houses and in the remaining 76 (43.68%) cases, the tutor comes to the students' houses (Table 4.5a,b,c).

Some of the sample students attend coaching classes both in the morning and evening hours. A school child feels over-strained by spending more than three hours on tuition in a day in addition to the time spent in school. A student will obviously feel tired by studying for hours together. A student requires some leisure time for relaxation. Replying to our question relating to the tuition timing of the sample students, it is recorded that, of the 174 sample students availing tuitions, 66 (37.93%) students attend tuitions in the morning hours, 21 (12.07%) go for the coaching classes during the afternoon, and 39 (22.41%) go for tuition classes during the evening hours. It is seen that 48 (27.59%)

Table 4.5a: Distribution of sample students in terms of going to tutor's house for coaching and sex [N=174]

Sex	*Going to Tutor's House for Coaching*		*Total*
	Yes	*No*	
Male	(75%) 72 (73.47%)	(25%) 24 (31.58%)	(100%) 96 (55.17%)
Female	(33.33%) 26 (26.53%)	(66.67%) 52 (68.42%)	(100%) 78 (44.83%)
Total	(56.32%) 98 (100%)	(43.68%) 76 (100%)	(100%) 174 (100%)

Table 4.5b: Distribution of sample students in terms of going to tutor's house for coaching and age group [N=174]

Age Group	*Going to Tutor's House for Coaching*		*Total*
	Yes	*No*	
< 12 Yrs.	(40%) 12 (12.24%)	(60%) 18 (23.68%)	(100%) 30 (17.24%)
13-14 Yrs.	(53.85%) 42 (42.86%)	(46.15%) 36 (47.37%)	(100%) 78 (44.83%)
> 15 Yrs.	(66.67%) 44 (44.9%)	(33.33%) 22 (28.95%)	(100%) 66 (37.93%)
Total	(56.32%) 98 (100%)	(43.68%) 76 (100%)	(100%) 174 (100%)

Table 4.5c: Distribution of sample students in terms of going to tutor's house for coaching and course affiliation [N=174]

Course Affiliation	*Going to Tutor's House for Coaching*		*Total*
	Yes	*No*	
ICSE	(67.16%) 45 (45.92%)	(32.84%) 22 (28.95%)	(100%) 67 (38.51%)
CBSE	(44.64%) 25 (25.51%)	(55.36%) 31 (40.79%)	(100%) 56 (32.18%)
HSC	(54.9%) 28 (28.57%)	(45.1%) 23 (30.26%)	(100%) 51 (29.31%)
Total	(56.32%) 98 (100%)	(43.68%) 76 (100%)	(100%) 174 (100%)

students attend coaching classes both in the morning and evening time (Table 4.6a,b). A male student of class VIII, studying in CSBZS says:

> "After returning from school, I attend two tuition classes which are far off from my house, that too in opposite directions. I cover roughly 4 kms. a day for attending my school and tuitions. I feel very tired both physically and mentally by the time I retire to bed."

Table 4.6a: Distribution of sample students in terms of sex and tuition timings [N=174]

Tuition Timings	*Sex*		*Total*
	Male	*Female*	
Morning	(36.36%) 24 (25%)	(63.64%) 42 (53.85%)	(100%) 66 (37.93%)
Afternoon	(80.95%) 17 (17.71%)	(19.05%) 04 (5.13%)	(100%) 21 (12.07%)
Evening	(71.79%) 28 (29.17%)	(28.21%) 11 (14.1%)	(100%) 39 (22.41%)
Morning and Evening	(56.25%) 27 (28.12%)	(43.75%) 21 (26.92%)	(100%) 48 (27.59%)
Total	(55.17%) 96 (100%)	(44.83%) 78 (100%)	(100%) 174 (100%)

Table 4.6b: Distribution of sample students in terms of age group and tuition timings [N=174]

Tuition Timings	*Age Group*			*Total*
	<12 Yrs.	*13-14 Yrs.*	*>15 Yrs.*	
Morning	(18.18%) 12 (40%)	(50%) 33 (42.31%)	(31.82%) 21 (31.82%)	(100%) 66 (37.93%)
Afternoon	(42.86%) 09 (30%)	(28.57%) 06 (7.7%)	(28.57%) 06 (9.09%)	(100%) 21 (12.07%)
Evening	(12.82%) 05 (16.67%)	(41.03%) 16 (20.5%)	(46.15%) 18 (27.27%)	(100%) 39 (22.41%)
Morning and Evening	(8.33%) 04 (13.33%)	(47.92%) 23 (29.49%)	(43.75%) 21 (31.82%)	(100%) 48 (27.59%)
Total	(17.24%) 30 (100%)	(44.83%) 78 (100%)	(37.93%) 66 (100%)	(100%) 174 (100%)

The remarks of Sudeep speak of how he feels disgusted. Going to school and then attending the coaching classes is a very tiring experience for him everyday. But he cannot help it. As a small boy of just 13 years, he gets exhausted and thus loses his mental stability and physical fitness at the end of the day. This may affect his health and make him weak.

It is a fact that, in our contemporary societies, if mornings are meant for school, then evenings are meant for tuitions. There is a tuition house in almost every corner of the street and this only goes to prove how much more overburdened the child is.

The nature of question papers is of high importance. Malpractice in examination is one of the main stumbling blocks in the qualitative progress of education. The present educational system in general and examination system in particular are highly disturbed and distorted due to unprecedented recourse to malpractice in various forms. The manner in which malpractice in examinations take their rightful place, there is no need for teaching, attending classes, teachers' preparation and research activities in the country (Mishra, 1994: 14). Emphasis on final examination at the end of the course becomes a heavy mental strain and fear of possible failure, which impels the pupils to take recourse of malpractice in examinations.

The introduction of periodic unit test increases the sincerity of both the students and teachers, as well as it reduces the mental burden of the students. In our study it is marked that the English medium schools conduct quarterly tests including the terminal and annual examinations. But the system of periodic unit test is yet to be introduced in the Oriya medium schools. In these schools the students appear the final examinations at the end of the year. The introduction of the monthly tests in the English medium schools is no doubt beneficial for the students, but it also becomes a burden for the students at the initial stage. The students find it difficult to be regular in revising their course and prepare for the unit tests. As soon as the session starts, the students have no time for relaxation as they have to be simultaneously sincere in the school work, tuition work and home work. But at a later stage during the final examinations their burden is reduced, as they are prepared before hand. For the students of Oriya medium schools, examinations become a tension, as they appear the final examinations at the end of the session. Most of the students are not sincere during the whole year and work very hard only a month before appearing the examinations. This creates a mental stress and strain for the students for which they adopt some unfair means, like malpractice during the examinations.

The question pattern for the examinations is another factor for consideration. In our study it is noticed that most of the questions are short type and the remaining of are objective type[4]. In these types of questions a student has to be very thorough in the subject. A student has to spend much of his time for in-depth study. It is seen that the sample students are made acquainted with these type of questions in their respective coaching classes. Whatever may be the pattern of examination, our sample students feel overburdened due to the difficulty level of the course curriculum. They find it hard to digest the new syllabus. In addition to the school hours, many students attend oaching classes. The present educational system has increased the 'udy hours of students many fold.

While path breaking, devoted teachers and attractive, innovative teaching techniques are great stimulants for schools to "pull in" greater number of children, the examination system has always had a dampening effect upon the students. Forced to be guessing about the probability of questions to be asked in examinations students get into rough-and-tumble with them and lose their personality in the process. Examination fever is a term very often mentioned during the time of examinations when boys and girls nervously prepare for their examination by mugging up lessons and memorizing the portions expected. Sleepless nights, tensions, worries and exhaustion are the heavy price the school children pay for the challenge of examinations. A question arises – why is the examination so frightening? And why do children not take examinations somewhat supportively and as a good challenge to show interest in? Some radical minded educationists call it a tyranny! It is observed that the examinations conducted in the sample schools truly circumscribe the cognitive abilities of the students to mere rot learning. They do not test the examinees capacity for original thinking. They are not concerned with analytical, descriptive and interpretative abilities of the students. They test only their capacity for vomiting out everything swallowed into the mind. The way examinations are being held does not help in strengthening the memory power but in overburdening it.

NOTES

1. By moratorium I mean a temporary ban.
2. These are assignments given to students on various topics in each subject. It

may include: collecting pictures, taking photographs, makings drawings, constructing models in a given topic.

3. This implies Mother Indian Language. The language Oriya is the mother tongue of the Oriyas and Hindi is the national language of India. These two languages as subject are compulsory in all the schools irrespective of any course affiliation in the State of Orissa.
4. By objective type I mean closed ended questions having multiple choices.

5

Students at School and Teachers' Expectations

The primary function of the school is to instruct children and the school-life is co-extensive with academic pursuits. The level of qualifications of teachers has improved and it could be the basis of improving the quality of teaching. However, the activities of the children at school are bureaucratized by the adult (Hartley, 1987: 47). "Children are the objects of the school enterprise, persons to whom actions are done; and, further that they are powerless to reconstruct the school as a social institution to meet their own ideas about what would constitute a child-friendly education setting. For them, the school is an impervious, congealed construction of social norms" (Mayall, 1994: 124). Compared to home life, life at school offers little scope for negotiation with the adults in authority. Children find themselves treated as group members rather than as individuals, and as objects of socialization rather than as participating people (*ibid.* 124). The adult has further knowledge of the school as ideal environment to ensure that children have no legitimate voice. The children never reach maturity or independence at school. The independence that teachers say they aim for in children turns out to be conformity with school norms, both academic and social (*ibid.* 122). Teachers impart teaching and training to the children within the framework of their understanding of the "good child" (*ibid.* 123).

The school has gradually taken over more and more of the functions of the home. Changed economic and social conditions in recent times have brought about big changes in the relative importance of the home and the school. This, of course, does not imply by any means division of responsibility between the home and the school. At almost every point the two overlap and nothing could be more frustrating for a child than the lack of unity and harmony between home life and his school life. The school assumes a greater responsibility and becomes an extension of the family and is not be divorced from it. Promotion of talent and quality is one of the main goals of any system of education.

School children are busy and occupied in preparing their class-room lessons, doing the home assignments, revising the course for examinations, participating in extra-curricular activities, taking extra-coaching and also helping their parents in some household work. Apart from these activities, which overburden them, the distance covered by the students to reach school makes them feel exhausted. Some children stay at far off places from the school. An analysis of the distance of the school from the house and the mode of conveyance has been made for a better understanding (Chart 8).

Chart 8: Distribution of sample students in terms of the distance covered by them to reach the school [N=240]

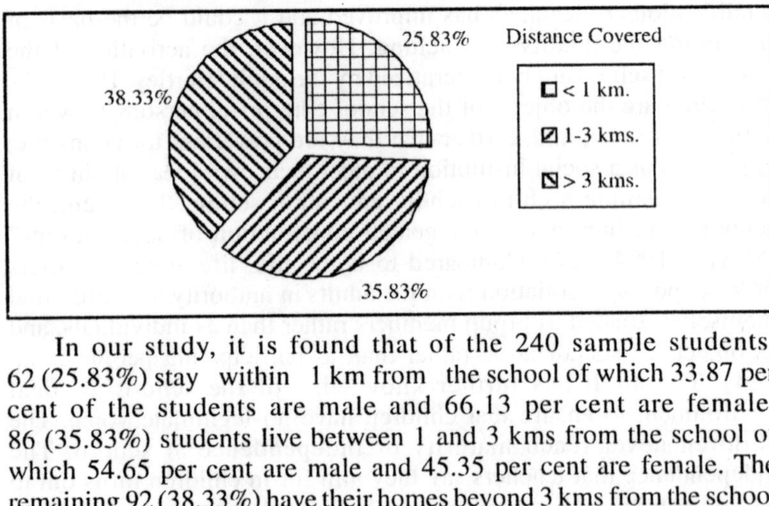

In our study, it is found that of the 240 sample students, 62 (25.83%) stay within 1 km from the school of which 33.87 per cent of the students are male and 66.13 per cent are female. 86 (35.83%) students live between 1 and 3 kms from the school of which 54.65 per cent are male and 45.35 per cent are female. The remaining 92 (38.33%) have their homes beyond 3 kms from the school of which 52 (52.52%) and 40 (43.48%) are male and female respectively (Table 5.1a). This shows that the highest percentage of students stay beyond 3 kms from the school. As regards the course affiliation, 45.00 per cent students of ICSE background stay beyond 3kms from the school. In case of CBSE background 61.25 per cent live beyond 3 km from the school. In case of students from HSC background, 51.25 per cent stay within 1 km from the school (Table 5.1b).

The mode of conveyance to reach the school has also been analyzed. Table 5.2a,b shows that of the 240 sample students, 84 (35.00%) go to school by bus, whereas 92 (38.33%) go by cycle

Table 5.1a: Distribution of sample students in terms of distance covered to reach the school and sex [N=240]

Sex	*Distance Covered to Reach the School*			*Total*
	< 1 km.	*1 km. – 3 km.*	*> 3 km.*	
Male	(17.5%) 21 (33.87%)	(39.17%) 47 (54.65%)	(43.33%) 52 (56.52%)	(100%) 120 (50%)
Female	(34.17%) 41 (66.13%)	(32.5%) 39 (45.35%)	(33.33%) 40 (43.48%)	(100%) 120 (50%)
Total	(25.83%) 62 (100%)	(35.83%) 86 (100%)	(38.34%) 92 (100%)	(100%) 240 (100%)

Table 5.1b: Distribution of sample students in terms of distance covered to reach the school and course affiliation [N=240]

Course Affiliation	*Distance Covered to Reach the School*			*Total*
	< 1 km	*1 km – 3 km*	*> 3 km*	
ICSE	(21.25%) 17 (27.42%)	(33.75%) 27 (31.4%)	(45%) 36 (39.13%)	(100%) 80 (33.33%)
CBSE	(5%) 04 (6.45%)	(33.75%) 27 (31.4%)	(61.25%) 49 (53.26%)	(100%) 80 (33.33%)
HSC	(51.25%) 41 (66.13%)	(40%) 32 (37.2%)	(8.75%) 07 (7.61%)	(100%) 80 (33.34%)
Total	(25.83%) 62 (100%)	(35.83%) 86 (100%)	(38.34%) 92 (100%)	(100%) 240 (100%)

and the remaining 64 (26.67%) go to school on foot. A further analysis shows that 43.33 per cent of female students go to school by bus and 40.00 per cent of male students go to school by cycle. It is found that of the 72 students of less than 12 years of the age, 19 (26.39%) go to school by bus, 27 (37.50%) go by cycle and the remaining 26 (36.11%) go to the school by walking. Of the 92 sample students between 13 and 14 years of age, 37 (40.22%) go to school by bus, 32 (34.78%) students go to school by cycle and one-fourth go by walking. Of the 76 students of more than 15 years of age, 28 (36.84%) students go to

Table 5.2a: Distribution of sample students in terms of availed mode of conveyance to reach school and sex [N=240]

Sex	*Availed Mode of Conveyance to Reach School*			*Total*
	Bus	*Cycle*	*Walking*	
Male	(26.67%) 32 (38.1%)	(40%) 48 (52.17%)	(33.33%) 40 (62.5%)	(100%) 120 (50%)
Female	(43.33%) 52 (61.9%)	(36.67%) 44 (47.83%)	(20%) 24 (37.5%)	(100%) 120 (50%)
Total	(35%) 84 (100%)	(38.33%) 92 (100%)	(26.67%) 64 (100%)	(100%) 240 (100%)

Table 5.2b: Distribution of sample students in terms of availed mode of conveyance to reach school and age group [N=240]

Age Group	*Availed Mode of Conveyance to Reach School*			*Total*
	Bus	*Cycle*	*Walking*	
< 12 Yrs.	(26.39%) 19 (22.62%)	(37.5%) 27 (29.35%)	(36.11%) 26 (40.62%)	(100%) 72 (30%)
13-14 Yrs.	(40.22%) 37 (44.05%)	(34.78%) 32 (34.78%)	(25%) 23 (35.94%)	(100%) 92 (38.33%)
> 15 Yrs.	(36.84%) 28 (33.33%)	(43.42%) 33 (35.87%)	(19.74%) 15 (23.44%)	(100%) 76 (31.67%)
Total	(35%) 84 (100%)	(38.33%) 92 (100%)	(26.67%) 64 (100%)	(100%) 240 (100%)

school by bus, 33 (43.42%) go by cycle and the remaining 15 (19.74%) go to school by walking (Table 5.2c).

It is noteworthy to make a comparison of the distance of the school from the home with the mode of conveyance to reach the school (Chart 9). Our data shows that of the 84 sample students going to school by bus, none stay within a radius of 1km from the school, 36 (42.86%) live at a distance between 1 and 3 kms from the school and 48 (57.14%) students stay beyond 3 kms from the school. Of the 92 students going to school by cycle, 16 (17.39%) stay within 1 km from the school, 38 (41.30%) stay between 1 and 3 kms from the school whereas 38 (41.30%) stay more than 3 kms from the school. Of the 64 sample students going to school by walking, 46 (71.88%) stay

Table 5.2c: Distribution of sample students in terms of availed mode of conveyance to reach school and course affiliation [N=240]

Course Affiliation	*Availed Mode of Conveyance to Reach School*			*Total*
	Bus	*Cycle*	*Walking*	
ICSE	(27.5%) 22 (26.19%)	(26.25%) 21 (22.83%)	(46.25%) 37 (57.81%)	(100%) 80 (33.33%)
CBSE	(65%) 52 (61.9%)	(31.25%) 25 (27.17%)	(3.75%) 03 (4.69%)	(100%) 80 (33.33%)
HSC	(12.5%) 10 (11.9%)	(57.5%) 46 (50%)	(30%) 24 (37.5%)	(100%) 80 (33.34%)
Total	(35%) 84 (100%)	(38.33%) 92 (100%)	(26.67%) 64 (100%)	(100%) 240 (100%)

Chart 9: Distribution of sample students in terms of their mode of conveyance to reach the school [N=240]

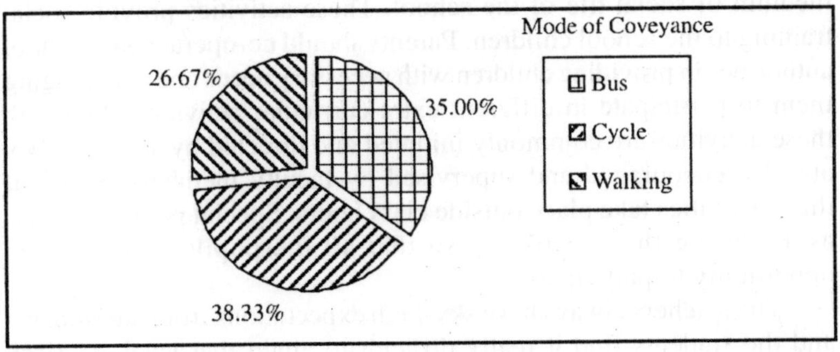

within a distance of 1 km 12 (18.75%) stay between 1 and 3 kms from the school, while the remaining 6 (9.38%) stay beyond 3 kms from the school (Table 5.2d).

School activities, outside regular classroom instruction, have been associated with formalized education. As a child grows, his interest in schoolwork increases simultaneously with his interest in games and sports. The non-academic activities are regarded as a by product of the regular school activity. These non-academic informal social

Table 5.2d: Distribution of sample students in terms of availed mode of conveyance to reach school and distance of school [N=240]

Distance of School	*Availed Mode of Conveyance to Reach School*			*Total*
	Bus	*Cycle*	*Walking*	
< 1 km	—	(25.81%) 16 (17.39%)	(74.19%) 46 (71.88%)	(100%) 62 (25.83%)
1 km to 3 km	(41.86%) 36 (42.86%)	(44.19%) 38 (41.3%)	(13.95%) 12 (18.75%)	(100%) 86 (35.83%)
> 3 km	(52.17%) 48 (57.14%)	(41.31%) 38 (41.3%)	(6.52%) 06 (9.37%)	(100%) 92 (38.34%)
Total	(35%) 84 (100%)	(38.33%) 92 (100%)	(26.67%) 64 (100%)	(100%) 240 (100%)

activities of the children in the school are termed as extra-curricular activities. The extra-curricular activities are the positive means of developing proper attitudes, habits and ideals of conduct through the medium of social life of the school. These activities provide social training to the school children. Parents should co-operate with school authorities in providing children with necessary needs and encouraging them to participate in different extra-curricular activities. Although these activities are commonly initiated and directed by students they are also encouraged and supervised by faculty members. Some of these activities take place outside class hours. Special periods are set-aside during the school day so that all the pupils may have an opportunity to participate.

The teachers always have sky-high expectations from the students and the students find it really difficult to attain that level. Matjcek (1985: 118) estimates that one-fifth to one-fourth of the child population finds itself under chronic stress with regard to school performance and achievement. This in part indicates the probable relation between the physical and the subjective time in school for this group of children. Various extra-curricular activities, *viz.* annual functions, games and sports, science exhibitions, debates, *Ganesh puja* and *Saraswati puja* are organized in the school under the leadership/supervision of the teachers. The Scout and NCC programmes managed by the school itself are no exceptions. The students are hardly given opportunity to participate in activities without the intervention of the seniors, particularly teachers. Apart from a good academic performance the teachers expect that students should always participate in the extra-curricular activities of the school. This is just loading burdens on a child's young shoulders (Graph 1).

Graph 1: Distribution of sample students in terms of their prime participation in extra-curricular activities [N=240]

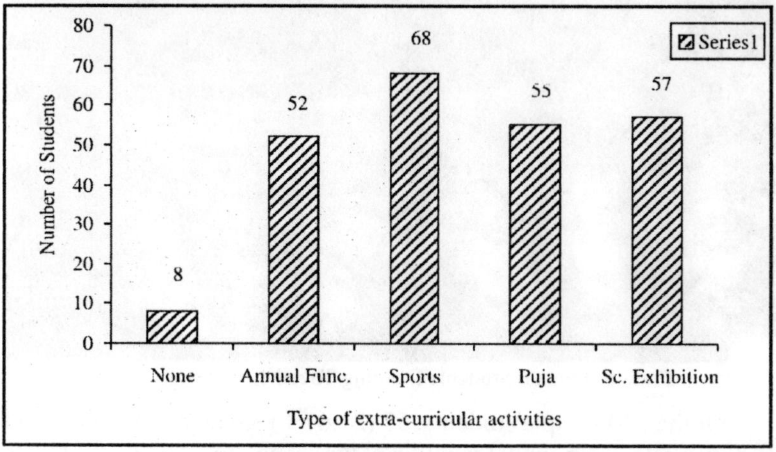

The child is dragged away from the street and shut up into a de-urbanized room, the school. The one as the other shaded from noise from the outside. What an enormous change for children who were used to freedom and free movements in the streets, who henceforth in their work and play are kept away from productive activities, deprived of own responsibility and subjected to rearing discipline. A whole, young, but previously active part of the population is transplanted from outside to inside (Aries, 1994: 65).

The main decrease in parental control has been brought about by the institutional pattern of childhood. Institutions[1] are controlling children's actions to a great extent. Institutionalization of childhood is the increasing influence exerted by educational institutions. There is a shift from informal to formal control. Institutionalization decreases parents' social control over children. A student sometimes participates in more than one extra-curricular activity in the school. An analysis has been made with regard to the primary interest of the students to participate in different extra-curricular activities (Plate 5).

Plate 5: Female Students Dancing Together in Annual Day

Of the 240 sample students, 52 (21.67%) are primarily interested to participate in the annual function of the school, 68 (28.33%) students are more inclined to participate in games and sports, 55 (22.92%) students are keen to participate in the *puja* activities, 57 (23.75%) have their prime interest in the participation in science exhibition conducted by the school and the remaining 8 (3.33%) do not participate in any of the extra-curricular activities of the school (Table 5.3a,b,c). A further analysis shows that, of the 96 high school[2] level students, the highest number of students. (*i.e.* 37.50 per cent) are interested to take part in science exhibition whereas of the 144 students at the M.E. level[3] 32.64 per cent are primarily interested in participating in games and sports (Table 5.3d). In our sample schools it is noticed that the participation of the children in the extra-curricular activities of the school is an indirect burden to the parents. Mostly during the *pujas* and in the annual day celebration money collection is done from the parents. This puts additional pressure on the parents through their children.

It is seen in our study that students participate in the extra-curricular activities of the school. In one of the cases it is noticed that one of the respondents made him over-involved in games and sports,

Table 5.3a : Distribution of sample students in terms of their sex and participation in prime extra-curricular activity [N=240]

Prime Extra-Curricular Activity	*Sex*		*Total*
	Male	*Female*	
None	(37.5%) 03 (2.5%)	(62.5%) 05 (4.17%)	(100%) 08 (3.33%)
Annual Function	(48.08%) 25 (20.83%)	(51.92%) 27 (22.5%)	(100%) 52 (21.67%)
Sports	(61.76%) 42 (35%)	(38.24%) 26 (21.67%)	(100%) 68 (28.33%)
Puja	(38.18%) 21 (17.5%)	(61.82%) 34 (28.33%)	(100%) 55 (22.92%)
Science Exhibition	(50.88%) 29 (24.17%)	(49.12%) 28 (23.33%)	(100%) 57 (23.75%)
Total	(100%) 120 (50%)	(100%) 120 (50%)	(100%) 240 (100%)

Table 5.3b: Distribution of sample students in terms of their age group and participation in prime extra curricular activity [N=240]

Prime Extra-Curricular Activity	*Age Group*			*Total*
	<12 Yrs.	*13-14 Yrs.*	*>15 Yrs.*	
None	(37.5%) 03 (4.17%)	(25%) 02 (2.17%)	(37.5%) 03 (3.95%)	(100%) 08 (3.33%)
Annual Function	(34.62%) 18 (25%)	(40.38%) 21 (22.83%)	(20%) 13 (17.11%)	(100%) 52 (21.67%)
Sports	(35.29%) 24 (33.33%)	(39.71%) 27 (29.35%)	(25%) 17 (22.37%)	(100%) 68 (28.33%)
Puja	(29.09%) 16 (22.22%)	(34.55%) 19 (20.65%)	(36.36%) 20 (26.31%)	(100%) 55 (22.92%)
Science Exhibition	(19.3%) 11 (15.28%)	(40.35%) 23 (25%)	(40.35%) 23 (30.26%)	(100%) 57 (23.75%)
Total	(30%) 72 (100%)	(38.33%) 92 (100%)	(31.67%) 76 (100%)	(100%) 240 (100%)

Table 5.3c: Distribution of sample students in terms of their course affiliation and participation in prime extra-curricular activity [N=240]

Prime Extra Curricular Activity	*Course Affiliation*			*Total*
	ICSE	*CBSE*	*HSC*	
None	(25%) 02 (2.5%)	(25%) 02 (2.5%)	(50%) 04 (5%)	(100%) 08 (3.33%)
Annual Function	(36.54%) 19 (23.75%)	(46.15%) 24 (30%)	(17.31%) 09 (11.25%)	(100%) 52 (21.67%)
Sports	(32.35%) 22 (27.5%)	(41.18%) 28 (35%)	(26.47%) 18 (22.5%)	(100%) 68 (28.33%)
Puja	—	(16.36%) 09 (11.25%)	(83.64%) 46 (57.5%)	(100%) 55 (22.92%)
Science Exhibition	(64.91%) 37 (46.25%)	(29.82%) 17 (21.25%)	(5.27%) 03 (3.75%)	(100%) 57 (23.75%)
Total	(33.33%) 80 (100%)	(33.33%) 80 (100%)	(33.34%) 80 (100%)	(100%) 240 (100%)

thereby neglected his studies. His deep involvement in sports led to the failure in his previous examination (Case Study 2).

Children are a lovely creation. The free time they get after a busy schedule of the day is chiefly responsible for the demand of recreation. Leisure is as important as work. Children feel tired after work and want to recreate themselves so as to gain efficiency. Leisure is the free time after the practical necessities of life have been attended to. Leisure is applied to slow, deliberate, unhurried undertakings. The use of this time is characterized by a high degree of personal freedom and choice. It is an opportunity to engage in some kind of activity, which is not required by daily necessity. Piaget and Inhelder (1979: 152) described the timings of school-going children as more orderly, structured and logical than that of a pre-school child. This emerging sense of order and logic enables children to play games with rules, thus providing more opportunities to consolidate previously learned skills and develop abilities that allow them to establish themselves within a peer group.

Table 5.3d: Distribution of sample students in terms of their educational standard and participation in prime extra-curricular activity [N=240]

Prime Extra Curricular Activity	*Educational Standard*		*Total*
	M.E. (Class-VI & VII)	*High Sch.(Class-VIII to X)*	
None	(37.5%) 03 (2.08%)	(62.5%) 05 (5.21%)	(100%) 08 (3.33%)
Annual Function	(73.08%) 38 (26.39%)	(26.92%) 14 (14.58%)	(100%) 52 (21.67%)
Sports	(69.12%) 47 (32.64%)	(30.88%) 21 (21.88%)	(100%) 68 (28.33%)
Puja	(63.64%) 35 (24.31%)	(36.36%) 20 (20.83%)	(100%) 55 (22.92%)
Science Exhibition	(36.84%) 21 (14.58%)	(63.16%) 36 (37.5%)	(100%) 57 (23.75%)
Total	(60%) 140 (100%)	(40%) 96 (100%)	(100%) 240 (100%)

The school children mostly like to spend their leisure with their peer group[4] or with brothers and sisters. A significant part of their remaining time children spend with their friends and schoolmates, with peers who are co-actors of vital importance for a major part of childhood. The peer group is usually a world apart. Stone and Chruch (1966: 118) stress the separation between the society of the gang of kids and the adult world. The gang of peers exists not only as an end in itself but also as a fortress, making it safe to test resistance to adult authority.

It is observed that in the school the students find it monotonous to sit continuously in a particular posture without talking to their classmates for six long hours. Sitting in an over-congested classroom with only a break-time of about 30 minutes makes them feel completely exhausted and tired. Further a high percentage of the students dislike the threatening environment in the school. Children always enjoy freedom. They do not like to be under domination or to be under restrictions. Especially when s/he attains the teen age s/he dislikes restrictions.

The educational system of our sample schools depicts an authoritarian rule. The administration takes its absolute right to lay down the criteria for judging the outcome of learning. In the words of John Stuart Mill – "The world already knows everything, and has only to tell it to its children". The school-going children do not have to think, explore, observe, analyze, conclude or discover. They just have to take it in. It was observed that the students are rarely asked to make independent observations. They are certainly never asked to judge the quality of the answers, either their own or those given in the book. It is clear then, that what takes place in the class-room implies knowledge as product of knowledgeable authorities. All of these lead to a view of both learning and knowledge as authority dependent.

The position of children in school, the relation between children and child workers is the other side of the problem. The "passive" interpretation of children's activities in school suggests the image of a factory (school) where raw materials (children) are transformed by workers (teachers) in finished goods (adults). Although this interpretation is unacceptable for everybody, I fear it is the most pertinent one. If school is for the betterment of the students, school culture would have to change drastically towards de-bureaucratization and towards introducing self-management of schools by children themselves.

In one of our sample schools the headmistress is a strict disciplinarian. She is very rigid about the rules and regulations of the school. She expects all the students to be punctual all the time. No student must be seen outside the classroom, except during the recess and game period. Though she is very co-operative by nature, she is very particular about all the activities of the students inside the school campus. It is observed that even during the game period or recess time when the students play in the playground, they do not like to play in front of some particular teachers. The presence of those teachers frightens them. Some teachers in the sample schools have a natural tendency to dominate the students. Those teachers not only restrict them within the classroom but also when they are outside in the playground. This leads them to a mental depression. A girl of class VIII, studying in SJCHS narrates:

> "I do not like the threatening/authoritarian environment that prevails in my school campus. I like freedom. My teachers hardly interact with me outside the classroom. I dislike the domination of the teachers in all children's activities."

As a matter of fact, the aforesaid statement indicates that Manisha is not satisfied with the suffocated atmosphere in the school. She feels that her teachers maintain a distance with her. She dislikes being under restrictions in all her activities in the school. It appears that the kind of freedom necessary for a healthy development of personality is not there in her school. This is quite depressing to her.

For children, the most natural, suitable and effective type of relaxation and regeneration of physical and mental capacities is moving about outdoors, "in the fresh air". The confined space of apartments and the limited possibilities for being outdoors in an environment corresponding to the developmental needs of children put city children at a disadvantage compared with rural children. Many young elementary school children's time to be outdoors consists primarily of playing on metal or plastic equipment and/or in a school yard stripped of tree cover or interesting vegetation. In fact, many schools in the United States have eliminated outdoor time in the form of recess (Clements, 2001: 96).

In our sample schools some of the students engaged themselves in playing indoor games like carom, chess, ludo, etc. while others play outdoor games like cricket, football, hide and seek, badminton and volley ball. Each class has two game periods in a week. Game materials are issued to the class monitors during the games periods. Some of the female students in the high school level get themselves engaged in embroidery and sewing. A few of the sample students spend their leisure in creative activities like drawing and painting *(Plate 6)*.

Plate 6: Students Playing During Break Time

Our study reveals that the students are not only under the domination of the teachers but also under many senior students in the school. The senior students in most of the cases are noticed exercising their power and rights over the junior students. This behaviour is particularly marked in the game period, when the game materials are issued to the class monitors. The senior students in many cases are seen availing the best chance. They first issue the better game equipments for their class and leave the rest for the junior classes. They also occupy a spacious area of the field for playing thereby restricting the junior students' area of playing. The senior students domination is also seen at the time of the annual day celebration, *puja* activities and functions during the Independence Day[5] and Republic Day[6]. The junior students are expected to work hard on these days in the school. The seniors instruct the juniors to carry out various tasks. Some are seen just bossing over the juniors unnecessarily. This behaviour and attitude make the junior students feel inferior.

The quality of education depends largely upon the quality of teachers. Of all the different factors that influence the quality of education, the competence and character of teachers are undoubtedly the most significant. The situation in a class, where the teacher just lectures and the students listen, is entirely different from the one where all the students take part in discussion. It is important to mention that all the teachers of the sample schools follow non-participatory method of teaching. A "monologue class room situation" is a common sight. A teacher has to spend more class-time raising questions and encouraging students to raise them and less time in "presenting the subject". A female student of MCPS studying in class IX states:

> "As an average student of my class, I do not receive adequate attention from my teachers. They do not seem to be concerned about me. They always give more importance to a few students who are exceptionally bright and are able to follow their lectures."

The above complaint of Monalisa brings to light the attitude of some teachers towards the average student. Quite often these students are under-estimated by their teachers. It also shows how such teachers teach at a very higher level, never coming down to the level of the average student. So the average students, who are at the receiving end, not only find the classroom environment threatening but also lose their interest in studies.

In our sample schools, it is observed that some of the teachers are partial in their judgment. They pay attention to the students on the basis of some criteria. They give unnecessary importance to brilliant students. They underestimate the dull students. Some teachers also differentiate the students according to their economic standard and thereby give attention to the students from the high-income group. Some teachers categorize students in accordance to their religious backgrounds. They exhibit indifferent attitude to students from other religious backgrounds. This creates a sort of mental depression in the minds of the students. They develop an inferiority complex within them, which disrupts their physical and intellectual development (Case Study 3).

Children are discriminated against on the basis of age. Their civil rights are routinely violated both at home and at school. Such deprivation prevents most of the children from reaching real maturity. When a good teacher-student relationship prevails in a school, a student feels free to discuss the problems s/he faces in the classroom teaching, course content, examinations, etc. When children are in difficulties the teacher solves their problem. Teachers' advice, co-operation and help are very crucial in creating a congenial environment in the school. The goals of the school, delivery of the curriculum, social norms and practices are founded on knowledge about the "facts" of child development. This set of understandings amongst school teachers is critical as far as children are concerned, because they find they are not taken seriously.

The welfare state plays a significant role in perpetuating the notion of childhood as a minority group and in concealing its social visibility (Makrinioti, 1994: 268). Oldman (1994: 44) claims that children constitute rather more than a minority group defined by an absence of rights, although minority status is certainly an emergent feature of childhood. He considers adult and children as constituting classes, in the sense of being social categories which exists principally by their economic opposition to each other and the ability of the dominant class (adults) to exploit economically the activities of the subordinate class (children).

Jaya Prakash Rao, the Principal of Satyam Public School states:

> "Unfortunately in Hyderabad, securing admissions into the schools remains the main focus. The main relevance of education, which is learning, is completely lost. All that parents and students of today are worried about the marks.

> Knowing the present scenario and the focus on marks, principals of schools today have become like film producers. They give what the audience wants. If the parents want only results, they ensure that and in the process take no steps to further the inner meaning of education, which is learning" (Internet Material).

Ranks, marks, grades, honours list become focus issues, not knowledge and certainly not wisdom. Children experience school as a competitive place rather than a co-operative place. Teachers often foment competition and competitive thinking assuming that such an approach leads to success. One of our sample schools makes children seated in the classroom in order of rank, changing it quite frequently. It is an educationally self-defeating and child-unfriendly procedure. The vision compounds with adult knowledge of the school as an ideal environment to ensure that children have no legitimate voice. The sample schools are over-administered by the teachers. The teachers take several decisions under the plea "in the best interest of the students". However, such administrative decisions are not child friendly. Rather those are directed towards controlling the children for the "best interest of teachers". The children never reach maturity or independence at school. The adult understanding and the rigid structure, framing and maintaining them, leave the children little scope for negotiation. The statement given by a male student of class VIII studying in CSBZS is as follows:

> "Our teachers think that we are just a nuisance and do not know anything. Their behaviour seems to be indifferent and rude. They often ask us to behave like adults forgetting that they themselves were children once."

The above statement given by Rakesh reflects his negative impression about the teachers. It seems that these teachers show no concern for their students. Instead they always measure children with standard that is right for the grown-ups and expect from them a much more mature behaviour which is impossible for a school child to fulfil. This makes them feel helpless.

In the sample schools it is noticed that not only the teachers observe students but also the students also minutely observe all the teachers. During their free time it is marked that they often discuss about the nature, behaviour and attitude of different teachers. The students are also seen watching their type of dress, hairstyle, gesture and posture. They are also particular about the mode of teaching and nature of punishment the teachers give. Taking into account some of the above criteria, sometime the students give a particular nickname to a teacher indicating some peculiar characteristics in him/her. The name giving is done normally with those teachers who are either very strict or do not impart effective teaching.

The data presented in Tables 5.4a,b show the behaviour of the classteachers towards the students in the school. Of the 240 sample students, 146 (60.83%) found their classteacher non-co-operative by nature. Only 94 (39.17%) students thought the class-teacher to be co-operative. Of the 94 students who like the behaviour of their class teacher, 47.87 per cent are from HSC background, 36.17 per cent are from CBSE background and 15.96 per cent are from ICSE background. On the other hand, of the 146 students who opined their class teacher as non-cooperative, 44.52 per cent are from ICSE background, 31.51 per cent are from CBSE background and the remaining 23.97 per cent are from HSC background (Table 5.4c). The best way to guarantee children's right is to promote their individual autonomy and the active construction of their own development. This implies that the school, together with the family, should fulfil the need and the corresponding right of children to move towards independence by participating in the construction of their own knowledge. Without doubt, we can affirm that the Convention clearly upholds, in Article 29, the Right of the Child to be educated in school for autonomy and liberty.

Table 5.4a: Distribution of sample students in terms of opinion on the behaviour of class teacher and sex [N=240]

Sex	*Behaviour of Class Teacher*		*Total*
	Co-operative	*Non-cooperative*	
Male	(46.67%) 56 (59.57%)	(53.33%) 64 (43.84%)	(100%) 120 (50%)
Female	(31.67%) 38 (40.43%)	(68.33%) 82 (56.16%)	(100%) 120 (50%)
Total	(39.17%) 94 (100%)	(60.83%) 146 (100%)	(100%) 240 (100%)

Table 5.4b: Distribution of sample students in terms of opinion on the behaviour of class teacher and age group [N=240]

Age Group	*Behaviour of Class Teacher*		*Total*
	Co-operative	*Non-cooperative*	
< 12 Yrs.	(36.11%) 26 (27.66%)	(63.89%) 46 (31.51%)	(100%) 72 (30%)
13-14 Yrs.	(41.3%) 38 (40.43%)	(58.7%) 54 (36.98%)	(100%) 92 (38.33%)
> 15 Yrs.	(39.47%) 30 (31.91%)	(60.53%) 46 (31.51%)	(100%) 76 (31.67%)
Total	(39.17%) 94 (100%)	(60.83%) 146 (100%)	(100%) 240 (100%)

Table 5.4c: Distribution of sample students in terms of opinion on the behaviour of class teacher and course affiliation [N=240]

Course Affiliation	*Behaviour of Class Teacher*		*Total*
	Co-operative	*Non-cooperative*	
ICSE	(18.75%) 15 (15.96%)	(81.25%) 65 (44.52%)	(100%) 80 (33.33%)
CBSE	(42.5%) 34 (36.17%)	(57.5%) 46 (31.51%)	(100%) 80 (33.33%)
HSC	(56.25%) 45 (47.87%)	(43.75%) 35 (23.97%)	(100%) 80 (33.34%)
Total	(39.17%) 94 (100%)	(60.83%) 146 (100%)	(100%) 240 (100%)

Discipline in a school usually means order and system in doing things, regularity and obedience to commands. Superficially a school is said to have good discipline if its pupils are obedient in class and stay clear of moral delinquency. What type of discipline is used depends upon the teachers' expectation from the child and the type of situations that prevail in the school? Many techniques are used to discipline children, some of which are good while others are likely to lead to unfavourable attitudes on the child. There are mounting evidences that discipline affects the child's social development. The students do not grow up emotionally secure. In claiming the legal and moral right to inflict punishment upon children, the school reinforces the idea of the child as being in "need" of a particular form of discipline. By virtue of its legal authority, the school is able to impose its decision upon the students. Majority of the students show their unwillingness to accept the "reconstruction" of what they should be.

Corporal/physical and other forms of humiliating and degrading punishment is a legalized and socially accepted form of violence against children which breach children's fundamental human rights to respect for their physical integrity and human dignity. Physical and humiliating punishment can take a number of forms, including two categories:

- *Physical Punishment*: includes hitting the child with the hand or with an object (such as a cane, belt, whip, etc.), shaking or pinching or pulling their hair, forcing a child to stay in an uncomfortable or undignified position or to take any excessive physical exercise.
- *Humiliating Punishment*: includes various forms such as psychological punishment, verbal abuse, isolation or ignoring the child.

Repeated punishment may make children stubborn and also ignore the punishment. Hence, the teacher should be aware of not only the nature of punishment given to the students but also the frequency of punishment. Expecting obedience from students is a natural tendency with the teachers and to be obedient is a natural obligation on the part of the students. Of the total number of 240 sample students, 70 (29.17%) reported that they frequently receive punishment at school, out of which 81.43 per cent are male students and 18.57 per cent are female students. 108 (45.00%) students stated that they occasionally receive punishment at school, of which 41.67 per cent are male and 58.33 per cent are female. The remaining 62 (25.83%) students stated that they never get punishment by their teachers at school, of which 29.03 per cent are male, whereas 70.97 per cent are female (Table 5.5a,b).

73 (50.69%) students at the M.E. level of education report that they occasionally receive punishment at school whereas of the

Table 5.5a: Distribution of sample students in terms of frequency of punishment received at school and sex [N=240]

Sex	*Frequency of Punishment Received at School*			*Total*
	Never	*Occasionally*	*Frequently*	
Male	(15%) 18 (29.03%)	(37.5%) 45 (41.67%)	(47.5%) 57 (81.43%)	(100%) 120 (50%)
Female	(36.67%) 44 (70.97%)	(52.5%) 63 (58.33%)	(10.83%) 13 (18.57%)	(100%) 120 (50%)
Total	(25.83%) 62 (100%)	(45%) 108 (100%)	(29.17%) 70 (100%)	(100%) 240 (100%)

Table 5.5b: Distribution of sample students in terms of frequency of punishment received at school and course affiliation [N=240]

Course Affiliation	*Frequency of Punishment Received at School*			*Total*
	Never	*Occasionally*	*Frequently*	
ICSE	(40%) 32 (51.61%)	(33.75%) 27 (25%)	(26.25%) 21 (30%)	(100%) 80 (33.33%)
CBSE	(32.5%) 26 (41.94%)	(41.25%) 33 (30.56%)	(26.25%) 21 (30%)	(100%) 80 (33.33%)
HSC	(5%) 04 (6.45%)	(60%) 48 (44.44%)	(35%) 28 (40%)	(100%) 80 (33.34%)
Total	(25.83%) 62 (100%)	(45%) 108 (100%)	(29.17%) 70 (100%)	(100%) 240 (100%)

Table 5.5c: Distribution of sample students in terms of frequency of punishment received at school and educational standard [N=240]

Educational Standard	*Frequency of Punishment Received at School*			*Total*
	Never	*Occasionally*	*Frequently*	
M.E. (Class-VI & VII)	(9.03%) 13 (20.97%)	(50.69%) 73 (67.59%)	(40.28%) 58 (82.86%)	(100%) 144 (60%)
H.S. (Class-VIII to X)	(50.04%) 49 (79.03%)	(36.46%) 35 (32.41%)	(12.5%) 12 (17.14%)	(100%) 96 (40%)
Total	(25.83%) 62 (100%)	(45%) 108 (100%)	(29.17%) 70 (100%)	(100%) 240 (100%)

96 sample students at the high school level, 49 (50.04%) stated that they never receive punishment at school (Table 5.6c). As regards the nature of punishment, of the 240 sample students, 52 (21.67%) students receive heavy punishment at school of which 84.62 per cent are male and only 14.38 per cent are female. 112 (46.67%) students said that they receive moderate degree of punishment at school, of which 50.89 per cent are male and 49.11 per cent are female. The rest 76 (31.67%) students reported that a light type of punishment is given to them at school of which three-fourth are female and one-fourth are male (Table 5.6a,c).

It is found from the above table that of the 72 sample students of less than 12 years of age, 16 (22.22%) receive heavy punishment at school, 37 (51.39%) get moderate degree of punishment and the remaining 19 (26.39%) stated that they receive light type of punishment. Of the 92 students between 13 ad 14 years of age, 29 (31.52%) receive heavy degree of punishment, 38 (41.30%) get moderate type of punishment whereas the remaining 25 (27.17%) of the students get light punishment at school. Of the 76 students of more than 15 years of age only 7 (9.21%) get heavy type of punishment, 37 (48.68%) receive moderate degree of punishment and the remaining 32 (42.11%) students reported that they receive light type of punishment at school (Table 5.6b).

During the study it is observed that in the sample schools, some teachers punish the students on a regular basis. It appears as if giving punishment has become their habit. Some students receive heavy punishment almost daily. This creates a negative impression on the

Table 5.6a: Distribution of sample students in terms of nature of punishment received at school and sex [N=240]

Sex	*Nature of Punishment Received at School*			*Total*
	Heavy	*Moderate*	*Light*	
Male	(36.67%) 44 (84.62%)	(47.5%) 57 (50.89%)	(15.83%) 19 (25%)	(100%) 120 (50%)
Female	(6.67%) 08 (14.38%)	(45.83%) 55 (49.11%)	(47.5%) 57 (75%)	(100%) 120 (50%)
Total	(21.67%) 52 (100%)	(46.67%) 112 (100%)	(31.66%) 76 (100%)	(100%) 240 (100%)

Table 5.6b: Distribution of sample students in terms of nature of punishment received at school and age group [N=240]

Age Group	*Nature of Punishment Received at School*			*Total*
	Heavy	*Moderate*	*Light*	
< 12 Yrs.	(22.22%) 16 (30.77%)	(51.39%) 37 (33.04%)	(26.39%) 19 (25%)	(100%) 72 (30%)
13-14 Yrs.	(31.53%) 29 (55.77%)	(41.3%) 38 (33.93%)	(27.17%) 25 (32.89%)	(100%) 92 (38.33%)
> 15 Yrs.	(9.21%) 07 (13.46%)	(48.68%) 37 (33.03%)	(42.11%) 32 (42.11%)	(100%) 76 (31.67%)
Total	(21.67%) 52 (100%)	(46.67%) 112 (100%)	(31.66%) 76 (100%)	(100%) 240 (100%)

Table 5.6c: Distribution of sample students in terms of nature of punishment received at school and course affiliation [N=240]

Course Affiliation	*Nature of Punishment Received at School*			*Total*
	Heavy	*Moderate*	*Light*	
ICSE	(11.25%) 09 (17.31%)	(62.5%) 50 (44.64%)	(26.25%) 21 (27.63%)	(100%) 80 (33.33%)
CBSE	(23.75%) 19 (36.54%)	(45%) 36 (32.14%)	(31.25%) 25 (32.89%)	(100%) 80 (33.33%)
HSC	(30%) 24 (46.15%)	(32.5%) 26 (23.22%)	(37.5%) 30 (39.48%)	(100%) 80 (33.34%)
Total	(21.67%) 52 (100%)	(46.67%) 112 (100%)	(31.66%) 76 (100%)	(100%) 240 (100%)

teachers. Receiving frequent punishment has made some students stubborn and aggressive by nature. It is noticed that many high school level students have protested against this pattern of punishment. But it is seen that the students who are studying in the lower classes are unable to express their feelings, so they remain under mental tensions during the school hours.

As a matter of fact the above analysis indicates the existing punishment patterns in our sample schools. No child is spared for any wrong doing. During the course of my interview a male student of class VIII studying in CSBZC narrated his feelings as this:

> "I hate the punishment pattern of my class teacher. He punishes us almost on a regular basis even if we are not at fault. He exercises his power as his daily duty."

The above-mentioned statement by Ashok indicates that he regularly passes through terrible mental tension during the school hours. It seems that his class teacher does not spare a single student for even the slightest mistake. The teacher is very harsh is his dealings. His attitude shows a fault finding tendency and giving punishment has become his habit. This creates a fear complex in the students. Instead of inspiring the students he has become an object of fear for students in the class. They are the objects of the school enterprise, persons to whom actions are done.

Expecting improvement from child, is necessary to encourage him/her besides scolding him/her. By getting consistent encouragement, a child gets inspiration towards his/her new ambition; s/he gets mental support and self-confidence. To enhance potentialities of child, nature of parents/teachers' efforts should be internal and external. Trying for enrolling the children in good and standard school, as well as in coaching classes is external encouragement. By these efforts, children automatically get encouraged. The children get encouragement if they are praised and awarded occasionally. By this, they get energized and with help of new enthusiasm they follow new aims.

The school teacher is to guide students to the source of knowledge, introduce them to methods of analyzing and evaluating information and develop in them the ability to think creatively and independently. A teacher cannot arouse interest in his students for anything in which he has no great interest himself. There has been change found in the curriculum content. It is necessary that the teacher should understand the chief features of the new course curriculum. Teaching is rooted in learning and the two can never be separated in the actual educational process. Teaching is causing to learn. Nothing has been taught until it has been learnt. In our sample schools it is noted that about two-third of the teachers find the course structure to be heavy. The revised curriculum includes additional papers and new topics. The course structure has not only become vast but also increasingly difficult. The old teachers are not acquainted with the reformed syllabus. An analysis has been done to study the teachers' opinion on the course structure with respect to the sample schools.

A total number of 150 teachers are interviewed from the sample schools, of which 96 (64.00%) teachers reported that the course structure is heavy. Of those 46 (39.58%) teachers are from ICSE background, 33.33 per cent are from CBSE background and the remaining 27.08 per cent are from HSC background. 42 (28.00%) teachers stated that the course structure of their school is moderate, of which 21.43 per cent are from ICSE background, 35.71 per cent are from CBSE background and 42.86 per cent are from HSC background. The remaining 12 (8.00%) opined that the course structure is light by nature, of which 25.00 per cent teachers are from ICSE background, 25.00 per cent are from CBSE background, whereas the remaining half are from HSC background.

During the study, a teacher narrated his feelings as thus:

> "I joined in this school with high hopes. I thought that it is a Government school, which would be having good infrastructure and proper teaching aids but it was a wrong imagination. Without adequate infrastructure the teaching quality is going down. This could be one of the reasons why affluent parents are reluctant to admit their children in this school."

This comment indicates the impression of a teacher of CSBZS about the condition of the school. It appears as if he is disheartened due to the inadequate teaching aids, ill-managed library and the poor infrastructure of the school. This condition makes him feel suffocated. He is gradually loosing his interest in teaching even at a young age.

The present educational system is such that it has brought the school activities inside the home. It is significant to listen the conversation of two students of class VIII in SJCHS when I happened to pass through the corridor. One of them was telling the other that – "I am very much fond of playing cricket but when I return from school I do not get time to play with my friends. My teachers give homework in every subject. The workload is so much so that I hardly get time to relax. Really I am mentally disgusted." In many cases it is observed that children are so time bound that they do not get leisure throughout the day.

The engagement of students in school activities does not remain confined to the school building. School penetrates into family life, and thus a struggle arises between two that seeks to pre-structure children's life, space and time (Kovaqik, 1994: 113). It is the school that determines how much time remains to the child. The school "intrudes into family life by means of homework, which often requires the assistance of parents" (*ibid.* 114). If one estimates for students in higher grades on an average of two hours of essential homework a day (and it may be even more), one finds that the workload of school children is sometimes greater than that of adults. In the sample schools homework is given to the students in almost all the subjects. The students feel disgusted to do homework daily. Co-operation of parents is required in connection with homework done by the students. If the parents are less educated, the students are deprived of the required guidance from the parents and thus seek the help of tutors or classmates.

Parents' participation in helping their children with homework and studies is a relatively little explored subject. Parents are, however, generally bad teachers of their children in so far as homework is concerned, perhaps because of their too-personal involvement in their children's achievements. Contacts between parents and children in the course of homework and study are actually structured and determined from outside and are often coloured by tension and nervousness. In SJCHS a male student of class IX states:

> "The volume of homework sometimes exceeds my physical and mental capacities. My teachers give home-task in every subject. The fear of being punished for not doing homework forces me to give it top priority back at home."

The above comment of Pankaj shows his mental fatigue. It seems that he gives much importance to completing his homework rather than learning his daily lessons. It is probable that in a period of 40 minutes his teacher consumes maximum time giving homework and in collecting the worked out task of his previous class. He appears to be very harsh on the slightest negligence in doing the home assignments by any student in the class. This makes him feel disgusted and tired.

The analysis in Table 5.7a clearly gives a picture on the opinion about the volume of homework in the different educational standard. Of the 240 sample students, 98 (40.83%) opined that the volume of homework is heavy, of which 46.94 per cent are of M.E. school level and 53.06 per cent are of high school level. 92 (38.33%) felt that the volume of homework is moderate, of which 73.91 per cent are of M.E. level and 26.09 per cent are of high school level. The remaining 50 (20.83%) students reported that the homework given at school is light by nature of which 60.00 per cent are of M.E. level and 40.00 per cent are of high school level. A further analysis has been done to consider various opinions of the students on the volume of homework with regards to the different course affiliation. The data collected reveals that of the 80 ICSE students, 52.50 per cent feel the volume of

Table 5.7a: Distribution of sample students in terms of volume of homework given to them and educational standard [N=240]

Educational Standard	*Volume of Homework*			*Total*
	Heavy	*Moderate*	*Light*	
M.E. (Class-VI & VII)	(31.94%) 46 (46.94%)	(47.22%) 68 (73.91%)	(20.84%) 30 (60%)	(100%) 144 (60%)
H.S. (Class-VIII to X)	(54.17%) 52 (53.06%)	(25%) 24 (26.09%)	(20.83%) 20 (40%)	(100%) 96 (40%)
Total	(40.83%) 98 (100%)	(38.33%) 92 (100%)	(20.84%) 50 (100%)	(100%) 240 (100%)

Table 5. 7b: Distribution of sample students in terms of volume of homework given to them and course affiliation [N=240]

Course Affiliation	*Volume of Homework*			*Total*
	Heavy	*Moderate*	*Light*	
ICSE	(52.5%) 42 (42.86%)	(30%) 24 (26.09%)	(17.5%) 14 (28%)	(100%) 80 (33.33%)
CBSE	(37.5%) 30 (30.61%)	(45%) 36 (39.13%)	(17.5%) 14 (28%)	(100%) 80 (33.33%)
HSC	(32.5%) 26 (26.53%)	(40%) 32 (34.78%)	(27.5%) 22 (44%)	(100%) 80 (33.34%)
Total	(40.83%) 98 (100%)	(38.33%) 92 (100%)	(20.84%) 50 (100%)	(100%) 240 (100%)

homework to be heavy, 30.00 per cent find the homework to be moderate, yet 17.50 per cent feel the volume of homework to be light by nature. Of the 80 CBSE students, 37.50 per cent feel the homework to be heavy, 45.00 per cent feel the volume of homework moderate and 17.50 per cent find the homework to be light. Of the 80 HSC students, 32.50 per cent feel the volume of homework given at school to be heavy by nature, 40.00 per cent feel it moderate and the remaining 27.50 per cent feel the volume of homework to be light by nature (Table 5.7b). Thus, it can be assumed that a higher percentage of students reported that the volume of homework given at school is heavy (Chart 10).

Chart 10: Distribution of sample students in terms of their opinion on volume of homework [N=240]

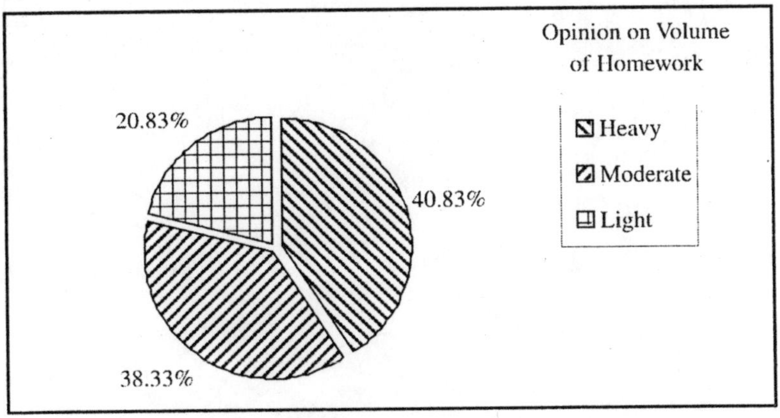

Have we ever given a thought to how overburdened children in today's age are? Have we ever given thought to the fact that they carry a heavy load in terms of education, expectations of the parents and society on their fragile shoulders? At our convenience we regard them as children, while expecting them to be adults most of the time. If all this sounds like fiction, it is not. It is a deep-rooted reality of today's educational system and society.

NOTES

1. I use the concept "institution" here in a more restricted way than the broad sociological concept meaning basis societal entities, in which the family is looked upon as an institution. I refer to organizations with goals, a work

organization, a structure of decision-making, a staff, etc. that have children as their main target group and staff members orientated towards work with children.

2. High School includes students of class VIII to class X.
3. M.E. (Middle Education) standard includes students of class VI and class VII.
4. Peer group means equal, *i.e.* friends of about the same age.
5. The Independence Day of India is celebrated on the 15th August.
6. India celebrates its Republic Day on the 26th January.

6

Students at Home and Parents' Expectations

A child when grows up is no longer a dependent child. The parents demand that s/he should act his/her age and try to confirm to adult standard of behaviour. They expect him/her to shoulder up some of the burdens at home. Parents value children's independent activity both as evidence that they are becoming capable, and to relieve the burden on themselves. Both children and their parents promote the view that children play an important part as agents in structuring and re-structuring the home as a social institution.

Children do not just belong to the family; they, to an extent, together with other family members, continuously create the family. They construct and refine relationships and social customs, and negotiate the division of labour within the home, settling conditionally for duties and freedoms and re-negotiating these over time. However, the involuntary participation of young children in household work and family occupations deprives them of "childhood" and its many opportunities, including those for schooling, recreation and rest (Nayar, 1991: 37).

In our sample area where labour is expensive, it is beyond the reach of many parents to employ full day servants for routine domestic work. The division of labour among the members of the family is the only solution to this problem. Thus the parents burden the children with domestic work. Parents generally do the responsible work and children assist them in their work. Parents usually have a differential attitude towards the sex role of their children. The criteria of age and sex are used while allotting the rights and duties. The boys are generally given the outside work but the girls assist their mothers in household works. Sample male students reported that they perform activities such as shopping, gardening and fetching portable water/milk. Female students stated that they get themselves engaged in activities like assisting in cooking, serving the food, sweeping, washing utensils, cleaning soiled clothes, attending to the guests, preparing the beds, watching the young ones. Looking after younger children of the family is a problem to all those families, which have dependent children. Working parents usually entrust the duty of looking after dependent children to older siblings. Goldscheider and Waite (1991: 96) observed the mothers, fathers and childrens from the same families. They argued for a reconceptualization of the division of labour as "three-cornered". Their investigation included an examination of which family members were typically responsible for specific household tasks.

It is observed among the sample students that most of them who come from extended families apart from their schoolwork are engaged in a few household activities in order to assist their parents. But students coming from nuclear families perform much household work at home due to the lack of support system. Such children are given many responsible and difficult tasks. In such familial setting usually the criteria of age and sex are no more taken into consideration, as there exists only few members. A male child having no sister replaces the work of her mother if she is ill. In many cases the parents assign such duties to their children, which become extra burden for them. In our study it is marked that some sample students of M.E. level are somewhat dissatisfied with the assigned home duties. They feel themselves too young to shoulder up the responsibilities given to them by their parents (Plate 7).

Plate 7: A School Child Engaged in Cleaning Utensils

It is noticed in our study that male students assist their parents in various non-domestic activities like: marketing, fetching portable water/milk. An interesting case is that a sample male respondent helps his father in business. He is now so much involved in learning various market policies and strategies that he fails to concentrate in his studies. He somehow rather wishes to complete his matriculation before starting a new business (Case Study 4).

In bringing up children, parents tend to be ambitious to make them achievers. There is pleading, persuasion, urging and even threat to enforce children's compliance of parental expectations. A surprisingly large proportion of the communication of parents to offspring consists of:

- Instruction on what to do,
- Motivating children to perform by offering rewards, and
- Threat of punishment, if performance does not reach the expected level.

The general belief is that competition is the only tool to make children achieve success in education. This view is so widely held that questioning it is considered unrealistic, eccentric or even deviant. The strategy in operation is competition. Wishing for the first rank, money, fame and success for the children is the general rule. So competition like charity begins at home. By the time the baby crawls to the door or lips the first syllables of language, the parents look out anxiously for any first-in-the class signs. Today's child does not have a childhood. There is a pressure on them to be achievers and performers. A young mother displays with pride, the medal her child gets in the kindergarten, treating it also as recognition of her talent as a mother. If the child does not get a similar medal in the next term, she blames herself. The close social circle also provides interaction and the consequent competition between children.

Sandhya, a student of class VII reports "My mom has been telling me from the day I joined school, that my only aim should be to become a doctor." Echoing Ranjit, a student of class VIII, who goes a step ahead to add that, "My father could not become an engineer because his parents did not have the money, but he tells me that I should become a software engineer and go to the US like the sons of his friends."

When I reached the doorstep of a respondent's house, I heard his mother shouting:

> "Mr. Pattnaik's (our neighbour) son secures the first position in the class but why is your position fourth? Bulu (Mr. Pattnaik's son) is equally outstanding in games and sports. He efficiently operates the computer, whereas you even do not match with him in these extra-curricular activities."

The above argument unearths the parental expectations. It seems as if Srideep's mother is over-concerned and worried about her son's rank as compared to his friend. This shows ranks, marks and grades have become her focus issue. The sky-high expectation to successfully combine studies with other activities is not an easy task. It is really difficult to attain that level. Further the comparison made by the parents may contribute to depression in their children. It is encouragement rather than comparison and fault finding that would help the children to grow intellectually.

Whether it is the comparative or superlative forms of adjectives, it is used several times in a day by the parents: "who finishes the homework first, can come with me to the shop". The child's world of language and conceptual awareness thus expands through comparison and contrast. The comparison of material objects and phenomena get extended to human beings, violating without warning the sense of uniqueness and individuality. And when comparison becomes an emotional whiplash in the hands of a powerful adult, the child's world crumbles. Familism and familization are the characteristics of welfare states' approach to childhood. From this perspective children and their needs cannot be defined independently of those of the family, nor can their needs be realized without the family. Children from this standpoint, fail to reach public as a social category and to establish their own existence as a distinct social entity. Many parents have demanding careers and fulfilment in their work is just as significant as fulfilment as a parent.

What is the outcome of such strong aspirations and drive of the parents? An over-burdened and over-worked child, who is undergoing a system of education to only fulfil the dreams of his parents or compete with his peers, not knowing whether he really wants to do so. While talking to some children in the age group of 12–15 years, some said that their ambitions were driven by their parents. Others felt that given a chance they would like to pursue some other line of their choice, but they love their parents too dearly to disappoint them.

It is found that the students try to show good results in examinations in order to fulfil the expectations of their parents. In spite of a busy schedule in a day, the students maintain proper study hours. An analysis has been done to find out the duration of study hours of children in a working day (Graph 2). Of the 240 sample

Graph 2: Distribution of sample students in terms of their course affiliation and duration of study hours in a working day [N=240]

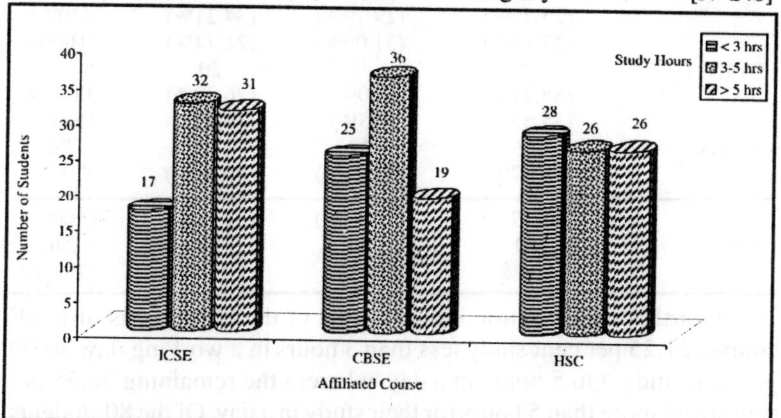

students, 70 (29.17%) study for less than 3 hours in a working day, of which 60.00 per cent are male and 40.00 per cent are female. 94 (39.17%) students study between 3 and 5 hours a day, of which 51.06 per cent are male and 48.94 per cent are female. 76 (31.67%) students put in more than 5 hours labour for their study in a working day, of which 39.47 per cent are male and 60.53 per cent are female (Tables 6.1a,b).

Table 6.1a: Distribution of sample students in terms of duration of study hours in a working day and sex [N=240]

Sex	*Duration of Study Hours in a Working Day*			*Total*
	< 3 hrs.	*3-5 hrs.*	*> 5 hrs.*	
Male	(35%) 42 (60%)	(40%) 48 (51.06%)	(25%) 30 (39.47%)	(100%) 120 (50%)
Female	(23.33%) 28 (40%)	(38.33%) 46 (48.94%)	(38.34%) 46 (60.53%)	(100%) 120 (50%)
Total	(29.17%) 70 (100%)	(39.17%) 94 (100%)	(31.66%) 76 (100%)	(100%) 240 (100%)

Table 6.1b: Distribution of sample students in terms of duration of study hours in a working day and age group [N=240]

Age Group	*Duration of Study Hours in a Working Day*			*Total*
	< 3 hrs.	*3-5 hrs.*	*> 5 hrs.*	
< 12 Yrs.	(25%) 18 (25.72%)	(38.89%) 28 (29.79%)	(36.11%) 26 (34.21%)	(100%) 72 (30%)
13-14 Yrs.	(27.17%) 25 (35.71%)	(51.09%) 47 (50%)	(21.74%) 20 (26.32%)	(100%) 92 (38.33%)
> 15 Yrs.	(35.53%) 27 (38.57%)	(25%) 19 (20.21%)	(39.47%) 30 (39.47%)	(100%) 76 (31.67%)
Total	(29.17%) 70 (100%)	(39.17%) 94 (100%)	(31.66%) 76 (100%)	(100%) 240 (100%)

A further investigation indicates that of the 80 students of ICSE course, 21.25 per cent study less than 3 hours in a working day, 40.00 per cent study 3 to 5 hours in a day, whereas the remaining 38.75 per cent spend more than 5 hours for their study in a day. Of the 80 students of CBSE course, 31.25 per cent read for less than 3 hours a day, 45.00 per cent study between 3 and 5 hours a day and 23.75 per cent spend more than 5 hours for their study in a day. Of the 80 students of HSC course, 35.00 per cent study less than 3 hours a day, 32.50 per cent study between 3 and 5 hours a day and the remaining 32.50 per cent of the students study for more than 5 hours a day (Table 6.1c).

Table 6.1c: Distribution of sample students in terms of duration of study hours in a working day and course affiliation [N=240]

Course Affiliation	*Duration of Study Hours in a Working Day*			*Total*
	< 3 hrs.	*3-5 hrs.*	*> 5 hrs.*	
ICSE	(21.25%) 17 (24.28%)	(40%) 32 (34.04%)	(38.75%) 31 (40.79%)	(100%) 80 (33.33%)
CBSE	(31.25%) 25 (35.72%)	(45%) 36 (38.3%)	(23.75%) 19 (25%)	(100%) 80 (33.33%)
HSC	(35%) 28 (40%) (29.17%)	(32.5%) 26 (27.66%) (39.17%)	(32.5%) 26 (34.21%) (31.66%)	(100%) 80 (33.34%) (100%)
Total	70 (100%)	94 (100%)	76 (100%)	240 (100%)

In some cases the students are unable to devote much time for their studies due to some unavoidable familial obligations. I came across with a case where the respondent's mother was bed-ridden owing to paralysis. For this reason the student had to shoulder up more domestic responsibilities. As a result she was not getting enough time for maintaining study hours (Case Study 5).

A separate room in the house is an essential requirement for a student in order to maintain the study hours. But this is practically not possible for many students in urban place like our study area where the city is over-congested and people stay in houses having limited rooms. Our study shows that as many as 60.83 per cent do not have their own study room and only 37.17 per cent have their own study room (Table 6.2a). Of the 94 students who have their own study room,

Table 6. 2a: Distribution of sample students in terms of provision of separate study room and sex [N=240]

Sex	*Provision of Separate Study Room*		*Total*
	Yes	*No*	
Male	(48.33%) 58 (61.7%)	(51.67%) 62 (42.47%)	(100%) 120 (50%)
Female	(30%) 36 (38.3%)	(70%) 84 (57.53%)	(100%) 120 (50%)
Total	(39.17%) 94 (100%)	(60.83%) 146 (100%)	(100%) 240 (100%)

48.94 per cent are from ICSE background. Of the 146 students who do not have a study room[1], 39.04 per cent are from HSC background (Table 6.2b). As regards the family size, 81.82 per cent students from large-sized family do not have their own study room (Table 6.2c). A girl of SJCHS studying in class IX tells:

> "There is always a rush of guests in my house. I do not remember of a single evening when guests have not crowded my house. I feel disturbed as I am unable to maintain my study hours."

The above reporting by Nibedita shows the non-congenial study atmosphere at her house. It appears that there is arrival of many family

Table 6.2b: Distribution of sample students in terms of provision of separate study room and course affiliation [N=240]

Course Affiliation	*Provision of Separate Study Room*		*Total*
	Yes	*No*	
ICSE	(57.5%) 46 (48.94%)	(42.5%) 34 (23.29%)	(100%) 88 (33.33%)
CBSE	(31.25%) 25 (26.6%)	(68.75%) 55 (37.67%)	(100%) 80 (33.33%)
HSC	(28.75%) 23 (24.46%)	(71.25%) 57 (39.04%)	(100%) 80 (33.34%)
Total	(39.17%) 94 (100%)	(60.83%) 146 (100%)	(100%) 240 (100%)

Table 6.2c: Distribution of sample students in terms of provision of separate study room and family size [N=240]

Family Size	*Provision of Separate Study Room*		*Total*
	Yes	*No*	
Small	(66.67%) 64 (68.09%)	(33.33%) 32 (21.92%)	(100%) 96 (40%)
Medium	(23.08%) 18 (19.15%)	(76.92%) 60 (41.1%)	(100%) 78 (32.5%)
Large	(18.18%) 12 (12.76%)	(81.82%) 54 (36.99%)	(100%) 66 (27.5%)
Total	(39.17%) 94 (100%)	(60.83%) 146 (100%)	(100%) 240 (100%)

friends and relatives in her house. It seems that the people who come there talk to one another loudly forgetting that they create disturbance to Nibedita. At times Nibedita's mother calls her to attend to the guests. This further disturbs her concentration leading to her poor performance in the examinations (Case Study 6).

For a student the home environment should be calm and peaceful. As a study room is essential for a student, so is the study atmosphere at home equally important for him/her. In order to prepare the school syllabus, complete the homework and revise the course for examinations a congenial atmosphere at home is an essential requirement for a student. If s/he does not get such an atmosphere during the morning/evening s/he is bound to continue his/her study up to late night. It becomes then over-strenuous for the child. Our study shows that of the 240 sample students, 78 (32.50%) have a congenial study atmosphere, of which 58.97 per cent are male and 41.03 per cent are female. 162 (67.50%) students do not have a congenial study atmosphere, of which 45.68 per cent are male and 54.32 per cent are female (Table 6.3a,b).

Table 6.3a: Distribution of sample students in terms of study atmosphere at home and sex [N=240]

Sex	*Study Atmosphere at Home*		*Total*
	Congenial	*Non-congenial*	
	(38.33%)	(61.67%)	(100%)
Male	46	74	120
	(58.97%)	(45.68%)	(50%)
	(26.67%)	(73.33%)	(100%)
Female	32	88	120
	(41.03%)	(54.32%)	(50%)
	(32.5%)	(67.5%)	(100%)
Total	78	162	240
	(100%)	(100%)	(100%)

Table 6.3b: Distribution of sample students in terms of study atmosphere at home and course affiliation [N=240]

Course Affiliation	*Study Atmosphere at Home*		*Total*
	Congenial	*Non-congenial*	
	(57.5%)	(42.5%)	(100%)
ICSE	46	34	80
	(58.97%)	(20.99%)	(33.33%)
	(13.75%)	(86.25%)	(100%)
CBSE	11	69	80
	(14.1%)	(42.59%)	(33.33%)
	(26.25%)	(73.75%)	(100%)
HSC	21	59	80
	(26.93%)	(36.42%)	(33.34%)
	(32.5%)	(67.5%)	(100%)
Total	78	162	240
	(100%)	(100%)	(100%)

Television in India exists in a complex social and cultural mosaic. Television is one of the most revolutionary inventions of the twentieth century. Its vast potentials as a powerful medium of mass communication cannot be undermined. The school-going children spend much of their valuable time in various activities in the home. Watching television is one of such activities by our sample students. The eye-catching programmes draw the attention and eagerness of the children. It forces them to spend many inactive hours sitting in front of the television. Time spent watching television is time taken away from other pursuits, such as playing, studying, keeping and renewing social contact. Television also throws in obscenity and violence for a good measure. The few good programmes on the small screen are also so hemmed in by attention-grabbing advertisements that even watching those programmes become a strain for the children. Channels like Star TV, ZEE TV, Aaj Tak, etc. have become great sources of attraction for the children.

Television is another intruder into family life. The most insatiable consumers of television seem to be school children. Television is in many cases the structuring factor of family evenings. There are, however, different ways of watching TV, one of which may give rise to critical and witty family conversation regarding a particular story or show. Watching TV, is not only a problem of spending too much time in front of TV but also a problem of getting used to serials lacking significant, meaningful and formative stories (Plate 8).

Plate 8: A Sample Student Watching Television

Television is an attraction both for the children and the adults (parents). During my visit to different houses I observed that switching on the TV has no particular time or any fixed time period. Each and every family member watches television whenever it is convenient to him or her. This has made the parents loose their control over their children. The programmes are so eye-catching that the parents are seen in front of the television for long time and therefore, they fail to restrict the children watching TV. Therefore, the children have developed a habit of watching the television even late in the night. Many students reported that they feel drowsy and uneasy in the classroom as they sleep late in the night after watching a movie. As they do not get sufficient rest in the night, they remain inattentive in the classroom and feel lazy throughout the day (Graph 3).

Graph 3: Distribution of sample students in terms of their age group and duration of watching TV [N=240]

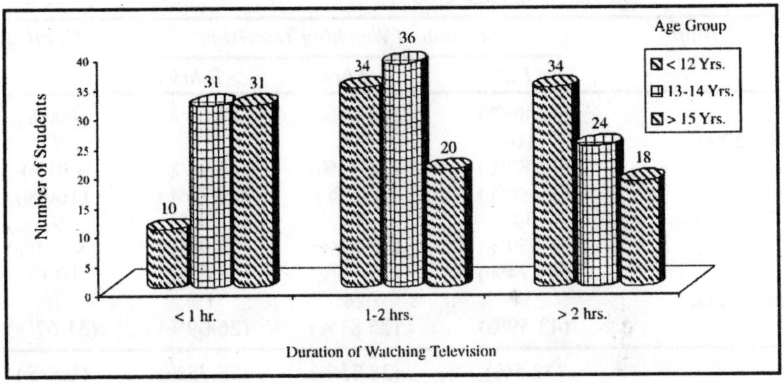

Our study reveals that of the 240 sample students, 78 (32.50%) spend less than 1 hour a day in watching TV, of which 12.82 per cent are less than 12 years of age, 43.59 per cent are in the age group 13-14 years and the remaining 43.59 per cent are more than 15 years of age. 93 (38.75%) students spend 1 to 2 hours in watching TV, of which one-third of the students are less than 12 years of age, 40.86 per cent students are between 13 and 14 years of age and one-fourth students are more than 15 years of age. The remaining 69 (28.75%) students spend more than 2 hours in watching TV, of which 44.93 per cent of the students are less than 12 years of age, 28.99 per cent students are in the age-group 13–14 years, whereas 26.09 per cent are more than 15 years of age (Table 6.4a,b,c).

Table 6.4a: Distribution of sample students in terms of duration of watching television and sex [N=240]

Sex	*Duration of Watching Television*			*Total*
	< 1 hr.	*1-2 hrs.*	*> 2 hrs.*	
Male	(46.67%) 56 (71.79%)	(35.83%) 43 (46.24%)	(17.5%) 21 (30.43%)	(100%) 120 (50%)
Female	(18.33%) 22 (28.21%)	(41.67%) 50 (53.76%)	(40%) 48 (69.57%)	(100%) 120 (50%)
Total	(32.5%) 78 (100%)	(38.75%) 93 (100%)	(28.75%) 69 (100%)	(100%) 240 (100%)

Table 6.4b: Distribution of sample students in terms of duration of watching television and age group [N=240]

Age Group	*Duration of Watching Television*			*Total*
	< 1 hr.	*1-2 hrs.*	*> 2 hrs.*	
< 12 Yrs.	(13.89%) 10 (12.82%)	(43.06%) 31 (33.33%)	(43.05%) 31 (44.93%)	(100%) 72 (30%)
13-14 Yrs.	(36.96%) 34 (43.59%)	(41.3%) 38 (40.86%)	(21.74%) 20 (28.98%)	(100%) 92 (38.33%)
> 15 Yrs.	(44.74%) 34 (43.59%)	(31.58%) 24 (25.81%)	(23.68%) 18 (26.09%)	(100%) 76 (31.67%)
Total	(32.5%) 78 (100%)	(38.75%) 93 (100%)	(28.75%) 69 (100%)	(100%) 240 (100%)

Despite several demerits of TV children also learn significantly from the television programmes. The visual image is bound to overshadow the spoken and the printed world. An analysis has been done with regard to the prime kind of programme a student likes to watch in a TV (Graph 4). Of the 240 sample students, 59 (24.58%) students watch primarily the news, 37 (15.42%) students watch primarily the UGC programme, 64 (26.67%) students watch primarily the serials, 28 (11.67%) are inclined to watch primarily the cartoon and children movies, the remaining 52 (21.67%) students are primarily interested in watching movies (Table 6.5a,b). Further analysis clearly indicates that maximum students of ICSE background are interested in watching

Table 6.4c: Distribution of sample students in terms of duration of watching television and course affiliation [N=240]

Course Affiliation	*Duration of Watching Television*			*Total*
	< 1 hr.	*1-2 hrs.*	*> 2 hrs.*	
ICSE	(40%) 32 (41.03%)	(47.5%) 38 (40.86%)	(12.5%) 10 (14.49%)	(100%) 80 (33.33%)
CBSE	(36.25%) 29 (37.18%)	(28.75%) 23 (24.73%)	(35%) 28 (40.58%)	(100%) 80 (33.33%)
HSC	(21.25%) 17 (21.79%)	(40%) 32 (34.41%)	(38.75%) 31 (44.93%)	(100%) 80 (33.34%)
Total	(32.5%) 78 (100%)	(38.75%) 93 (100%)	(28.75%) 69 (100%)	(100%) 240 (100%)

Graph 4: Distribution of sample students in terms of their sex and prime kind of programme they watch in TV [N=240]

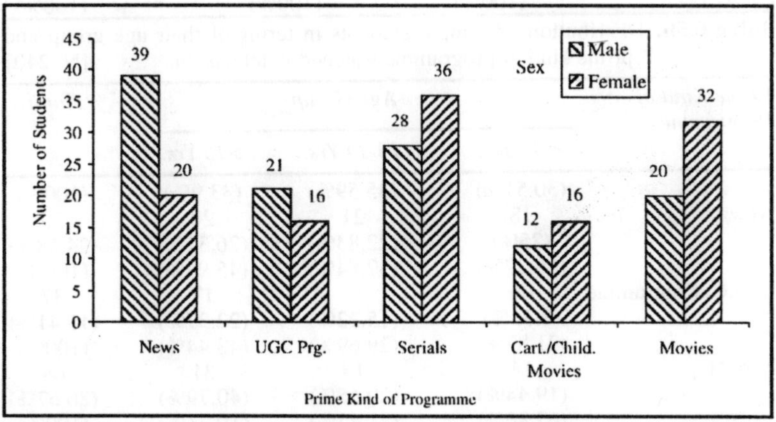

the news in TV. More number of CBSE students are found to be basically inclined towards the serials. Maximum numbers of students of HSC background have prime interest in watching movies (Table 6.5c).

For the school-going children it is essential to watch the daily news in the television. Students must have sufficient awareness about the current national and international events. Our study shows that of the total sample students, about one-fourth are interested in watching

Table 6.5a: Distribution of sample students in terms of their sex and prime kind of programme watched in television [N=240]

Prime Kind of Programme	*Sex*		*Total*
	Male	*Female*	
News	(66.1%) 39 (32.5%)	(33.9%) 20 (16.67%)	(100%) 59 (24.58%)
U.G.C. Programme	(56.76%) 21 (17.5%)	(43.24%) 16 (13.33%)	(100%) 37 (15.41%)
Serials	(43.75%) 28 (23.33%)	(56.25%) 36 (30%)	(100%) 64 (26.67%)
Cartoon/Children Movies	(42.86%) 12 (10%)	(57.14%) 16 (13.33%)	(100%) 28 (11.67%)
Movies	(38.46%) 20 (16.67%)	(61.54%) 32 (26.67%)	(100%) 52 (21.67%)
Total	(50%) 120 (100%)	(50%) 120 (100%)	(100%) 240 (100%)

Table 6.5b: Distribution of sample students in terms of their age group and prime kind of programme watched in television [N=240]

Prime Kind of Programme	*Age Group*			*Total*
	< 12 Yrs.	*13-14 Yrs.*	*>15 Yrs.*	
News	(30.51%) 18 (25%)	(35.59%) 21 (22.83%)	(33.9%) 20 (26.31%)	(100%) 59 (24.58%)
U.G.C. Programme	(16.22%) 06 (8.33%)	(37.84%) 14 (15.22%)	(45.94%) 17 (22.37%)	(100%) 37 (15.41%)
Serials	(21.87%) 14 (19.44%)	(29.69%) 19 (20.65%)	(48.44%) 31 (40.79%)	(100%) 64 (26.67%)
Cartoon/ Children Movies	(67.86%) 19 (26.89%)	(21.43%) 06 (6.52%)	(10.71%) 03 (3.95%)	(100%) 28 (11.67%)
Movies	(28.85%) 15 (20.83%)	(61.54%) 32 (34.78%)	(9.61%) 05 (6.58%)	(100%) 52 (21.67%)
Total	(30%) 72 (100%)	(38.33%) 92 (100%)	(31.67%) 76 (100%)	(100%) 240 (100%)

Table 6.5c : Distribution of sample students in terms of their course affiliation and prime kind of programme watched in television [N=240]

Prime Kind of Programme	*Course Affiliation*			*Total*
	ICSE	*CBSE*	*HSC*	
	(38.98%)	(27.12%)	(33.9%)	(100%)
News	23	16	20	59
	(28.75%)	(20%)	(25%)	(24.58%)
	(32.43%)	(51.35%)	(16.22%)	(100%)
U.G.C. Programme	12	19	06	37
	(15%)	(23.75%)	(7.5%)	(15.41%)
	(26.56%)	(37.5%)	(35.94%)	(100%)
Serials	17	24	23	64
	(21.25%)	(30%)	(28.75%)	(26.67%)
	(64.29%)	(21.43%)	(14.28%)	(100%)
Cartoon/ Children Movies	18	06	04	28
	(22.5%)	(7.5%)	(5%)	(11.67%)
	(19.23%)	(28.85%)	(51.92%)	(100%)
Movies	10	15	27	52
	(12.5%)	(18.75%)	(33.75%)	(21.67%)
	(33.33%)	(33.33%)	(33.34%)	(100%)
Total	80	80	80	240
	(100%)	(100%)	(100%)	(100%)

the news. An analysis has been done to ascertain the language of the news programme they watch in the television. Table 6.6a,b reveals that of the 59 sample students watching news, 18 (30.51%) students watch the news in English, 26 (44.07%) students watch news in Hindi and the remaining 15 (25.42%) students watch Oriya news. It is observed that of the 18 students who like watching English news, two-third of them are from ICSE background, 11.11 per cent are from CBSE background and 22.22 per cent are from the HSC background. Of the 26 students who primarily watch Hindi news, a little more than one-third are from ICSE background, a little less than half are from CBSE background and the remaining 19.23 per cent are from HSC background. Of the 15 students who primarily watch Oriya news, 13.33 per cent are from ICSE background, an identical percentage of students are from CBSE background whereas 73.33 per cent are from HSC background (Graph 5). Thus, it is observed that more number of students following the ICSE course primarily watch English news. Students from CBSE course are more inclined for the Hindi news

Table 6.6a: Distribution of sample students in terms of prime medium of language of the news watched in television and sex [N=59]

Sex	*Prime Medium of Language Watched in Television*			*Total*
	English	*Hindi*	*Oriya*	
Male	(33.33%) 13 (72.22%)	(48.72%) 19 (73.08%)	(17.95%) 07 (46.67%)	(100%) 39 (66.1%)
Female	(25%) 05 (27.78%)	(35%) 07 (26.92%)	(40%) 08 (53.33%)	(100%) 20 (33.9%)
Total	(30.51%) 18 (100%)	(44.07%) 26 (100%)	(25.42%) 15 (100%)	(100%) 59 (100%)

Table 6.6b: Distribution of sample students in terms of prime medium of language of the news watched in television and age group [N=59]

Age Group	*Prime Medium of Language Watched in Television*			*Total*
	English	*Hindi*	*Oriya*	
< 12 Yrs.	(22.23%) 04 (22.22%)	(44.44%) 08 (30.77%)	(33.33%) 06 (40%)	(100%) 18 (30.5%)
13-14 Yrs.	(19.05%) 04 (22.22%)	(57.14%) 12 (46.15%)	(23.81%) 05 (33.33%)	(100%) 21 (35.6%)
> 15 Yrs.	(50%) 10 (55.56%)	(30%) 06 (23.08%)	(20%) 04 (26.67%)	(100%) 20 (33.9%)
Total	(30.51%) 18 (100%)	(44.07%) 26 (100%)	(25.42%) 15 (100%)	(100%) 59 (100%)

whereas more numbers of students from HSC course prefer to watch news in Oriya (Table 6.6c).

The new social communication environment – the global information network Internet – imposed a new form of collaboration among the mass media. This environment, unique in itself, turned out to be fraught with risk mainly for children. Children occupy a new kind of social space in the Net. They form a specific society and are the founders of a new "digital nation"[2]. They link with each other all over the world without their parents' help, share on-line culture, games,

Graph 5: Distribution of sample students in terms of their course affiliation and prime language of news they watch in TV [N=59]

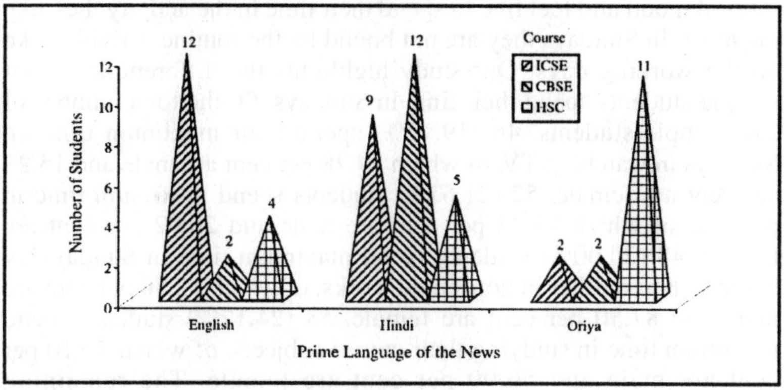

Table 6.6c: Distribution of sample students in terms of prime medium of language of the news watched in television and course affiliation [N=59]

Course Affiliation	*Prime Medium of Language Watched in Television*			*Total*
	English	*Hindi*	*Oriya*	
ICSE	(52.17%) 12 (66.67%)	(39.13%) 09 (34.62%)	(8.7%) 02 (13.33%)	(100%) 23 (38.98%)
CBSE	(12.5%) 02 (11.11%)	(75%) 12 (46.15%)	(12.5%) 02 (13.33%)	(100%) 16 (27.12%)
HSC	(20%) 04 (22.22%)	(25%) 05 (19.23%)	(55%) 11 (73.34%)	(100%) 20 (33.9%)
Total	(30.51%) 18 (100%)	(44.07%) 26 (100%)	(25.42%) 15 (100%)	(100%) 59 (100%)

software and learn to be socially responsible (Katz, 1996). It is obvious that more and more netizens[3] have the feeling of living in houses with doors opened constantly. Anyone who wants to, could enter. Children are the most defenseless occupants of this "houses". And when the number of cases of intolerant behaviour and unawareness of the other goes up, many parents begin to claim the civil rights of them and their kids.

After a busy schedule, the students need some relaxation at the weekend. Sunday is a holiday and the school children remain in a relaxed mood and feel free to spend their time in the activity they like the most. In Sundays they are not bound by the routine activities like on the working days. Our study highlights the different ways our sample students spend their time in Sundays. Of the total number of 240 sample students, 46 (19.17%) spend their maximum time on Sundays in watching TV, of which 84.78 per cent are male and 15.22 per cent are female. 52 (21.67%) students spend maximum time in playing, of which 73.08 per cent are male and 26.92 per cent are female. 48 (20.00%) students spend maximum time in Sundays by helping their mother in household works, of which 12.50 per cent are male and 87.50 per cent are female. 58 (24.17%) students spend maximum time in studying their course subjects, of which 43.10 per cent are male and 56.90 per cent are female. The remaining 36 (15.00%) spend maximum time on Sunday by reading magazines and storybooks of which one-third are male and two-third are female (Table 6.7a,c). It is further interesting to note that maximum students those who spend most of their time in playing on Sundays are less than 12 years of age, maximum students who spend their time in

Table 6.7a: Distribution of sample students in terms of their sex and ways of spending maximum time on Sundays [N=240]

Way of Spending Max. Time	*Sex*		*Total*
	Male	*Female*	
Watching T.V.	(84.78%) 39 (32.5%)	(15.22%) 07 (5.83%)	(100%) 46 (19.17%)
Playing	(73.08%) 38 (31.67%)	(26.92%) 14 (11.67%)	(100%) 52 (21.67%)
Household Work	(12.5%) 06 (5%)	(87.5%) 42 (35%)	(100%) 48 (20%)
Studying	(43.1%) 25 (20.83%)	(56.9%) 33 (27.5%)	(100%) 58 (24.16%)
Reading Magazines/ Story Books	(33.33%) 12 (10%)	(66.67%) 24 (20%)	(100%) 36 (15%)
Total	(50%) 120 (100%)	(50%) 120 (100%)	(100%) 240 (100%)

watching TV are in the age group 13–14 years. Maximum students who are more than 15 years of age primarily help their mother in doing household works in Sundays (Table 6.7b).

Table 6.7b: Distribution of sample students in terms of their age group and ways of spending maximum time on Sundays [N=240]

Way of Spending Max. Time	*Age Group*			*Total*
	< 12 Yrs.	*13-14 Yrs.*	*>15 Yrs.*	
	(46.65%)	(47.83%)	(6.52%)	(100%)
Watching T.V.	21	22	03	46
	(29.17%)	(23.92%)	(3.95%)	(19.17%)
	(50%)	(38.46%)	(11.54%)	(100%)
Playing	26	20	06	52
	(36.11%)	(21.74%)	(7.89%)	(21.67%)
	(8.33%)	(31.25%)	(60.42%)	(100%)
Household Work	04	15	29	48
	(5.56%)	(16.3%)	(38.16%)	(20%)
	(27.59%)	(34.48%)	(37.93%)	(100%)
Studying	16	20	22	58
	(22.22%)	(21.74%)	(28.95%)	(24.16%)
	(13.89%)	(41.67%)	(44.44%)	(100%)
Reading Magazines/	05	15	16	36
Story Books	(6.94%)	(16.3%)	(21.05%)	(15%)
	(30%)	(38.33%)	(31.67%)	(100%)
Total	72	92	76	240
	(100%)	(100%)	(100%)	(100%)

Our study reveals that though Sunday is a holiday at the weekend, the child is not seen free, rather s/he is engaged in various activities. It is noticed that apart from the school studies, sample students from Christian background also attend Sunday schools[4] on Sunday. They follow a prescribed syllabus and appear half-yearly and annual examinations at the end of the year. It is also seen that the Punjabi sample students go to the Gurdwara every Saturday for some moral teachings. Many girls of higher age group are noticed observing fasting on certain days of a week. All these make them feel more exhausted. A female student of class X, studying in MGHS states:

> "I live in a joint family. My mother has a lot of familial obligations and domestic engagements. She expects me to help her in the household work, when I come back from school and also during holidays. Therefore, I do not get enough time to play with my friends."

Table 6.7c: Distribution of sample students in terms of their course affiliation and ways of spending maximum time on Sundays [N=240]

Way of Spending Max. Time	*Course Affiliation*			*Total*
	ICSE	*CBSE*	*HSC*	
Watching T.V.	(41.31%) 19 (23.75%)	(30.43%) 14 (17.5%)	(28.26%) 13 (16.5%)	(100%) 46 (19.17%)
Playing	(26.93%) 14 (17.5%)	(40.38%) 21 (26.25%)	(32.69%) 17 (21.25%)	(100%) 52 (21.67%)
Household Work	(35.42%) 17 (21.25%)	(22.92%) 11 (13.75%)	(41.66%) 20 (25%)	(100%) 48 (20%)
Studying	(31.03%) 18 (22.5%)	(24.14%) 14 (17.5%)	(44.83%) 26 (32.5%)	(100%) 58 (24.16%)
Reading Magazines/ Story Books	(33.33%) 12 (15%)	(55.56%) 20 (25%)	(11.11%) 04 (5%)	(100%) 36 (15%)
Total	(33.33%) 80 (100%)	(33.33%) 80 (100%)	(33.34%) 80 (100%)	(100%) 240 (100%)

The experience of Sanjukta unearths her role in the family management. It appears that her mother expects a lot more from her. Apart from her school and tuition hours, she spends a great deal of her time assisting her mother. Since she lives in a traditional joint family her mother is bound by many rules and obligations. Sometimes Sanjukta feels disgusted in assisting her mother in domestic works. This robs Sanjukta away from her childhood.

It is observed that most of the female sample students above 14 years of age assist their mothers in domestic activities like, sweeping, cleaning utensils, washing clothes, assisting in cooking, taking care of younger siblings (if any). Some are also seen doing work like, fetching milk, fetching portable water, etc. Families having better economic standard engage maid servants for assistance but the situation of families from the lower and middle-income groups is quite different. In such families the girls assist their mothers. This is a common pattern in case of families of our sample respondents from the HSC background (Graph 6).

The school children enjoy the most during vacations. It is a period of relaxation after a long time of routine work like school studies,

Graph 6: Distribution of sample students in terms of their sex and ways of spending maximum time on Sundays [N=240]

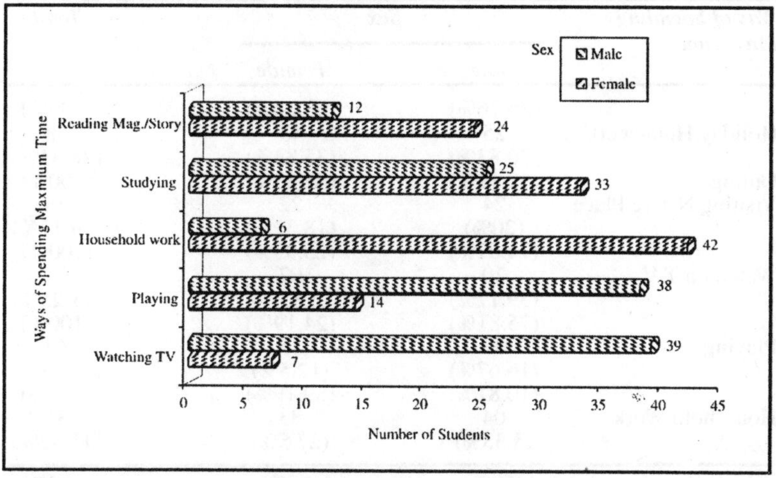

tuitions, extra-coaching, etc. However, it is noticed that the sample children of English Medium Schools are not even spared with from academics during vacations. They are assigned with heavy holiday homework[5] by their teachers. Of the 240 sample students, 68 (28.33%) spend maximum time during vacation in doing the holiday homework, 46 (19.17%) students spend their vacations by going for outings or visiting their native place, 27 (11.25%) spend much of their time during vacations in watching different programmes in the television, 62 (25.83%) students spend maximum time in playing and the remaining 37 (15.42%) utilize much of their time in assisting their mothers in different household activities (Table 6.8a,b). A further analysis reflects that maximum students of ICSE background reported that they spend much of their vacation time in doing holiday homework. Maximum students of CBSE background said that they spend their time in playing during vacations. Maximum students from the HSC background stated that they go for outing during the vacations (Table 6.8c).

The educational process is such that the school children are caught between the scylla of school regimentation and charybdis of parental authoritarianism. In our sample schools textbooks of the next higher class are being taught after completing the portions of the current year, here children are overburdened with no time left for rest and

Table 6.8a: Distribution of sample students in terms of their sex and ways of spending maximum time during vacations [N=240]

Way of Spending Max. Time	*Sex*		*Total*
	Male	*Female*	
	(36.76%)	(63.24%)	(100%)
Holiday Homework	25	43	68
	(20.83%)	(35.83%)	(28.33%)
Outing/	(52.17%)	(47.83%)	(100%)
Visiting Native Place	24	22	46
	(20%)	(18.33%)	(19.17%)
	(74.07%)	(25.93%)	(100%)
Watching T.V.	20	07	27
	(39.17%)	(5.83%)	(11.25%)
	(75.81%)	(24.19%)	(100%)
Playing	47	15	62
	(16.67%)	(12.5%)	(25.83%)
	(10.81%)	(89.19%)	(100%)
Household Work	04	33	37
	(3.33%)	(27.5%)	(15.42%)
	(50%)	(50%)	(100%)
Total	120	120	240
	(100%)	(100%)	(100%)

Table 6.8b: Distribution of sample students in terms of their age group and ways of spending maximum time during vacations [N=240]

Way of Spending Max. Time	*Age Group*			*Total*
	< 12 Yrs.	*13-14 Yrs.*	*>15 Yrs.*	
	(11.76%)	(38.24%)	(50%)	(100%)
Holiday Homework	08	26	34	68
	(11.11%)	(28.26%)	(44.74%)	(28.33%)
	(71.73%)	(21.74%)	(6.53%)	(100%)
Outing/ Visiting	33	09	03	46
Native Place	(45.83%)	(10.87%)	(3.95%)	(19.17%)
	(51.85%)	(33.33%)	(14.82%)	(100%)
Watching T.V.	14	10	04	27
	(19.44%)	(9.78%)	(5.26%)	(11.25%)
	(22.58%)	(67.74%)	(9.68%)	(100%)
Playing	14	42	06	62
	(19.44%)	(45.66%)	(7.89%)	(25.83%)
	(8.11%)	(13.51%)	(78.38%)	(100%)
Household Work	03	05	29	37
	(4.17%)	(5.43%)	(38.16%)	(15.42%)
	(30%)	(38.33%)	(31.67%)	(100%)
Total	72	92	76	240
	(100%)	(100%)	(100%)	(100%)

Table 6.8c: Distribution of sample students in terms of their course affiliation and ways of spending maximum time during vacations [N=240]

Way of Spending Max. Time	*Course Affiliation*			*Total*
	ICSE	*CBSE*	*HSC*	
Holiday Homework	(47.06%) 32 (40%)	(36.76%) 25 (31.25%)	(16.18%) 11 (13.75%)	(100%) 68 (28.33%)
Outing/ Visiting Native Place	(26.09%) 12 (15%)	(21.74%) 10 (12.5%)	(52.17%) 24 (30%)	(100%) 46 (19.17%)
Watching T.V.	(40.74%) 11 (13.75%)	(14.82%) 04 (5%)	(44.44%) 12 (15%)	(100%) 27 (11.25%)
Playing	(30.65%) 19 (23.75%)	(45.16%) 28 (35%)	(24.19%) 15 (18.75%)	(100%) 62 (25.83%)
Household Work	(16.22%) 06 (7.5%)	(35.13%) 13 (16.25%)	(48.65%) 18 (22.5%)	(100%) 37 (15.42%)
Total	(33.33%) 80 (100%)	(33.33%) 80 (100%)	(33.34%) 80 (100%)	(100%) 240 (100%)

relaxation. At home the parents start keeping their wards during summer holidays engaged in studying the next year's textbooks. Children are thus denied the freedom of enjoying their holidays in the company of nature and occupying themselves in fun, plan and excursions (Graph 7).

Graph 7: Distribution of sample students in terms of their educational standard and ways of spending maximum time during vacations [N=240]

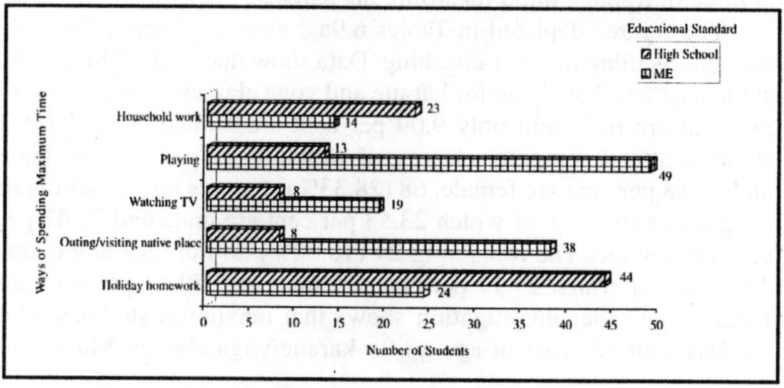

Children are categorized as "super kids" by their parents, because basically they press their children to excel, particularly in academic pursuits. Besides acceleration, children are required to strive for super academic excellence. Children are expected to be equally outstanding in music, sports, dance, arts and social discourse. Thus, in addition to tuition for their studies, some of them have instructors for swimming, music, computers, karatte and public speaking. These courses are pursued not for the child's enjoyment or relaxation, but for attaining more merits or distinctions, as desired by the parents. The child's routine consists of round of classes, instruction and coaching. Though it is good to learn something extra, yet it increases the workload of the already overburdened child. Such children find it really difficult to combine their studies, tuitions, homework and the extra-coaching simultaneously and successfully. It is seen that some of the sample students cover a long distance both for going to school and taking extra-coaching. As a result, they get exhausted physically and mentally. A male student of class IX studying in MCPS narrates thus:

> "I feel exhausted as I find it difficult to match with the expectations of my parents. My parents are always bossing me about. They fuss much and dish out too much advice. I cannot always be bothered to do everything they wish".

This reflects Rahul's feelings towards his parents. It is likely that he often feels irritated by listening to his parents' suggestions and advices. It appears that they expect super excellence from Rahul both in academic and non-academic spheres. This shows that they are over-concerned about him. This has gradually brought in a negative attitude in Rahul's mind regarding his parents.

The figures depicted in Tables 6.9a,c gives a picture of sample students availing of extra-coaching. Data show that of the 240 sample students, 66 (27.50%) go for karatte and yoga classes, of which 90.91 per cent are male and only 9.09 per cent are female. 82 (34.17%) students attend computer classes, of which 45.12 per cent are male and 54.88 per cent are female. 68 (28.33%) students take coaching in song/dance (music), of which 23.53 per cent are male and 76.47 per cent are female. The remaining 24 (10.00%) do not take any extra-coaching, of which 29.17 per cent are male and 70.83 per cent are female. A further investigation shows that maximum students who are less than 12 years of age go for karatte/yoga classes. Maximum

Table 6.9a: Distribution of sample students in terms of their sex and receiving extra-coaching in various fields [N=240]

Extra-Coaching	*Sex*		*Total*
	Male	*Female*	
No Extra- Coaching	(29.17%) 07 (5.83%)	(70.83%) 17 (14.17%)	(100%) 24 (10%)
Song/Dance	(23.53%) 16 (13.33%)	(76.47%) 52 (43.33%)	(100%) 68 (28.33%)
Computers	(45.12%) 37 (30.83%)	(54.88%) 45 (37.5%)	(100%) 82 (34.17%)
Karatte/Yoga	(90.91%) 60 (50%)	(9.09%) 06 (5%)	(100%) 66 (27.5%)
Total	(50%) 120 (100%)	(50%) 120 (100%)	(100%) 240 (100%)

Table 6.9b: Distribution of sample students in terms of their age group and receiving extra-coaching in various fields [N=240]

Extra-Coaching	*Age Group*			*Total*
	< 12 Yrs.	*13-14 Yrs.*	*>15 Yrs.*	
No Extra-Coaching	(54.17%) 13 (18.06%)	(29.17%) 07 (7.61%)	(16.66%) 04 (5.26%)	(100%) 24 (10%)
Song/Dance	(33.83%) 23 (31.94%)	(36.76%) 25 (27.17%)	(29.41%) 20 (26.31%)	(100%) 68 (28.33%)
Computers	(14.63%) 12 (16.67%)	(39.02%) 32 (34.78%)	(46.34%) 38 (50%)	(100%) 82 (34.17%)
Karatte/ Yoga	(36.36%) 24 (33.33%)	(42.42%) 28 (30.43%)	(21.22%) 14 (18.42%)	(100%) 66 (27.5%)
Total	(30%) 72 (100%)	(38.33%) 92 (100%)	(31.67%) 76 (100%)	(100%) 240 (100%)

numbers of students in the 13–14 and more than 15 years age groups attend computer classes (Table 6.9b). It appears that parents put in

Table 6.9c: Distribution of sample students in terms of their course affiliation and receiving extra-coaching in various fields [N=240]

Extra-Coaching	*Course Affiliation*			*Total*
	ICSE	*CBSE*	*HSC*	
No Extra-Coaching	(33.33%) 08 (10%)	(4.17%) 01 (1.25%)	(62.5%) 15 (18.75%)	(100%) 24 (10%)
Song/Dance	(29.41%) 20 (25%)	(30.88%) 21 (26.25%)	(39.71%) 27 (33.75%)	(100%) 68 (28.33%)
Computers	(37.8%) 31 (38.75%)	(35.37%) 29 (36.25%)	(26.83%) 22 (27.5%)	(100%) 82 (34.17%)
Karatte/ Yoga	(31.82%) 21 (26.25%)	(43.94%) 29 (36.25%)	(24.24%) 16 (20%)	(100%) 66 (27.5%)
Total	(33.33%) 80 (100%)	(33.33%) 80 (100%)	(33.34%) 80 (100%)	(100%) 240 (100%)

attempt to make their children genius at the earliest possible time (Graph 8).

Graph 8: Distribution of sample students in terms of their sex and receiving extra-coaching [N=240]

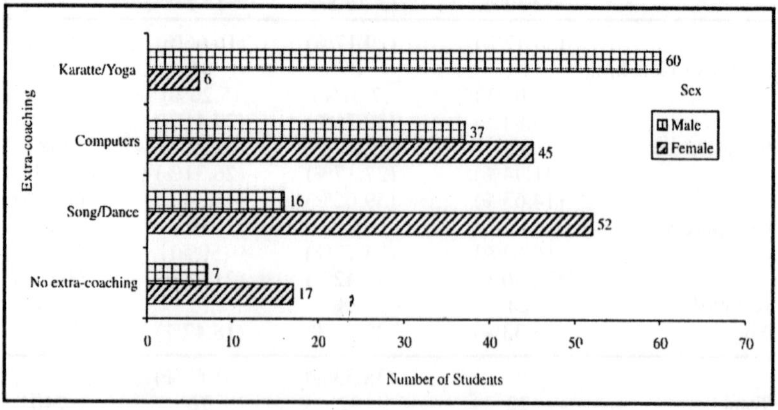

Taking extra-coaching is no doubt an additional burden to the students. However, some students do not take such extra-coaching for one or the other reason. I came across with one such students who in our study it is seen that a sample student though having the eager is deprived of taking extra-coaching as she is a polio patient. She is mentally a bit depressed compared to her classmates (Case Study 7).

Parents depend upon educational institutions for the educational progress of their children. However, at the same time they are to a great extent responsible for creating interest in their children and thus motivating them to achieve education. However, the school children are guided mostly by the attitude and aspirations of their parents. The children are allowed by parents to float in the stream of educational system, but how they are steered to reach their goals depends on the parents who hold the oars in their hands. Epstein (1995:235) conceptualized a framework of parents' involvement, which is learning at home and helping families to create home environments that support children's academic progress. This broad view of involvement affirms the parents' role as the child's primary teacher and the home as the child's first classroom. Parents have realized the necessity of educating their children for their future career, which suits this industrially developing country. Schools have multiplied and the urban parents are in touch with the educational system, which can give their children the necessary qualifications for their aspired career.

Parents with better educational background are able to give better guidance to their children. They are capable of developing the interest of their children in their school education through various means. In some cases it is found that the elder brother/sister or uncle/aunty also assists the sample students in their studies back at home. There are also some students who do not get assistance from anyone at home. The data analyzed in Tables 6.10a,b provide the categories of kin from whom sample students receive assistance in their studies at home. From among the total sample students, 68 (28.33%) get help from their fathers at home, of which 41.18 per cent are from ICSE background, 33.82 per cent are from CBSE background and one-fourth are from HSC background. 32 (13.33%) students receive assistance from their mothers back at home, of which 18.75 per cent belong to ICSE background, the same percentage of students are from CBSE background and 62.50 per cent are from HSC background. 47 (19.58%) students get assistance both from their fathers and mothers, of which 46.81 per cent are from ICSE background, 21.28 per cent are from CBSE background and a little less than one-third are from HSC background. 51 (21.25%) students receive help from their elder brother/sister, of which 15.67 per cent are from ICSE background, 56.86 per cent are from CBSE background, whereas

Table 6.10a: Distribution of sample students in terms of their course affiliation and help received in their study at home from different family members [N=240]

Categories of Helper	*Course Affiliation*			*Total*
	ICSE	*CBSE*	*HSC*	
None	(55%) 11 (13.75%)	(25%) 05 (6.25%)	(20%) 04 (5%)	(100%) 20 (8.33%)
Father	(41.18%) 28 (35%)	(33.82%) 23 (28.75%)	(25%) 17 (21.25%)	(100%) 68 (28.33%)
Mother	(18.75%) 06 (13.33%)	(18.75%) 06 (7.5%)	(62.5%) 20 (25%)	(100%) 32 (13.33%)
Both Father and Mother	(46.81%) 22 (27.5%)	(21.28%) 10 (12.5%)	(31.91%) 15 (18.75%)	(100%) 47 (19.58%)
Elder Brother/Sister	(15.69%) 08 (10%)	(56.86%) 29 (36.25%)	(27.45%) 14 (17.5%)	(100%) 51 (21.25%)
Any Other Uncle/Aunty	(22.13%) 05 (6.25%)	(31.82%) 07 (8.75%)	(45.45%) 10 (12.5%)	(100%) 22 (9.17%)
Total	(33.33%) 80 (100%)	(33.33%) 80 (100%)	(33.34%) 80 (100%)	(100%) 240 (100%)

27.45 per cent are of HSC background. 22 (9.17%) students are assisted by their uncle/aunty in their studies at home, of which 22.73 per cent are from ICSE background, 31.82 per cent are from CBSE background and little less than half are from HSC background. The remaining 20 (8.30%) students do not receive help in their studies from anyone at home, of which 55.00 per cent are from ICSE background, one-fourth belong to CBSE background and the remaining 20.00 per cent are from HSC background. Children who are appropriately supervised and guided have a better chance to be equipped physically, mentally, emotionally and socially. Children can concentrate in their study only when they stay in a congenial environment (Graph 9).

Our study shows that those sample students who are from a poor economic background do not perform well in the examinations. In many cases it is noticed that they do not get proper guidance from

Table 6.10b: Distribution of sample students in terms of their educational standard and help received in their study at home from different family members [N=240]

Categories of Helper	*Educational Standard*		*Total*
	ME (Class-VI & VII)	*High Sch.(Class-VIII to X)*	
None	(60%) 12 (8.33%)	(40%) 08 (8.33%)	(100%) 20 (8.33%)
Father	(47.06%) 32 (22.22%)	(52.94%) 36 (37.5%)	(100%) 68 (28.33%)
Mother	(78.13%) 25 (17.36%)	(21.87%) 07 (7.29%)	(100%) 32 (13.33%)
Both Father & Mother	(40.43%) 19 (13.19%)	(59.57%) 28 (29.17%)	(100%) 47 (19.58%)
Elder Brother/Sister	(78.43%) 40 (27.78%)	(21.57%) 11 (11.46%)	(100%) 51 (21.25%)
Any other Uncle/Aunty	(72.73%) 16 (11.11%)	(27.27%) 06 (6.25%)	(100%) 22 (9.17%)
Total	(60%) 144 (100%)	(40%) 96 (100%)	(100%) 240 (100%)

Graph 9: Distribution of sample students in terms of their age group and help they receive from different family members at home [N=240]

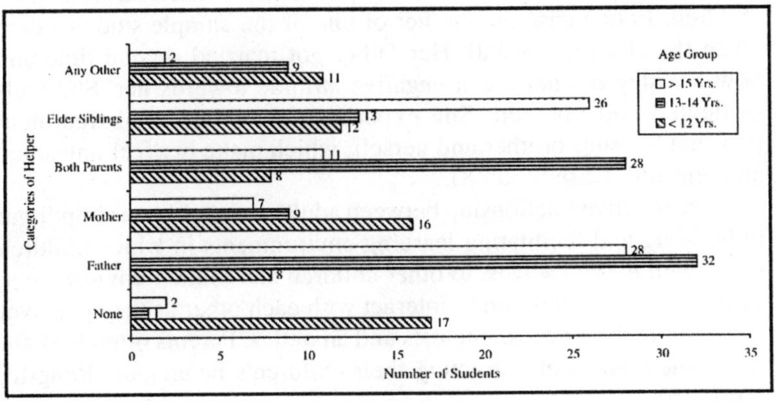

their parents, as their parents are not from better educational standards. As the parents are not financially sound, some of them fail to afford sending their children to attend coaching classes. As a result that makes those students feel inferior as compared to other students in the school. Sometimes it is also observed that some teachers show an indifferent attitude towards the students from poor economic background. This hurt the sentiments of those students and thereby brings in mental depression.

Parents must maintain a healthy attitude and affectionate behaviour towards their children. The effect of parental behaviour depends on the way in which the child perceives the parents, i.e. the meaning that their behaviour has for him. Children who have a good basic relation with their parents approve their parents' behaviour, whilst those who have a negative attitude towards their parents tend to object to almost any behaviour of the parents. More than the child's obedience and good behaviour the parents expect the child's good performance in their school examination. They usually hold high aspiration about their child's academic performance. The child keeps up to their expectations because he has high regards for them and their attitudes. Table 6.11a,b gives a clear picture of the student's opinion on the nature of concern of their parents towards them. Our study reveals that of the 240 sample students, 212 (88.33%) reported that their parents are concerned about them, of which 43.23 per cent are male students and 53.77 per cent are female students. 28 (11.67%) students opined that they have un-concerned parents, of which 78.57 per cent are male students and 21.43 per cent are female students.

Our study shows that maximum parents are concerned about their children. In one case the mother of one of our sample students died when the child was small. Her father got married second time and now her step-mother has a negative attitude towards her. She feels neglected and uncared. She experiences a differential treatment between her step-brother and herself, which make her feel unwanted and uncared (Case Study 8).

An affective relationship between adults and children is important in building and facilitating learning environments in which children relate well to themselves, to other children and to their environment. This encourages children to interact with each other as they discover and explore their needs, interests and anxieties. Parents often look for less violent ways of correcting their children's behaviour (Rengifo, 2003: 26).

Table 6.11a: Distribution of sample students in terms of their opinion on the nature of involvement of their parents and sex [N=240]

Sex	*Nature of Involvement of Parents*		*Total*
	Concerned	*Un-concerned*	
Male	(81.66%) 98 (46.23%)	(18.34%) 22 (78.57%)	(100%) 120 (50%)
Female	(95%) 114 (53.77%)	(5%) 06 (21.43%)	(100%) 120 (50%)
Total	(88.33%) 212 (100%)	(11.67%) 28 (100%)	(100%) 240 (100%)

Table 6.11b: Distribution of sample students in terms of their opinion on the nature of involvement of their parents and age group [N=240]

Age Group	*Nature of Involvement of Parents*		*Total*
	Concerned	*Un-concerned*	
< 12 Yrs.	(88.89%) 64 (30.19%)	(11.11%) 08 (28.57%)	(100%) 72 (30%)
13-14 Yrs.	(92.39%) 85 (40.09%)	(7.61%) 07 (25%)	(100%) 92 (38.33%)
> 15 Yrs.	(82.89%) 63 (29.72%)	(17.11%) 13 (46.23%)	(100%) 76 (31.67%)
Total	(88.33%) 212 (100%)	(11.67%) 28 (100%)	(100%) 240 (100%)

The school children should be taken care and proper attention must be given for their physical and intellectual development. No doubt parents are much concerned about their academic performance but attention should also be given towards their proper diet and good health. Children in general feel hungry after the long monotonous classroom teaching. They expect light refreshment during the recess period. This should be taken care by their mothers. An analysis has been made with regard to the type of tiffin taken by the sample students at school. Of a total number of 240 sample students, 82 (34.17%) take cooked tiffin to the school, of which 62.20 per cent are male and

37.80 per cent are female. 90 (37.50%) students go to school carrying ready-made tiffin, of which 37.78 per cent are male and 62.22 per cent are female. 28 (11.67%) students do not take tiffin-box along with them to the school but they use to buy some food items from the mobile stalls, of which about two-third are male and one-third are female. 24 (10.00%) students go to their respective home during the recess period for tiffin, of which 20.83 per cent are male and 79.17 per cent are female. The remaining 16 (6.67%) students neither take any kind of tiffin at school nor do they go back home for tiffin, of which 68.75 per cent are male and 31.25 per cent are female (Table 6.12a,b).

Table 6.12a: Distribution of sample students in terms of their sex and type of tiffin they take to school [N=240]

Type of Tiffin at School	*Sex*		*Total*
	Male	*Female*	
No Tiffin	(68.75%) 11 (9.17%)	(31.25%) 05 (4.17%)	(100%) 16 (6.67%)
Cooked Tiffin	(62.2%) 51 (42.5%)	(37.8%) 31 (25.83%)	(100%) 82 (34.17%)
Ready-made Tiffin	(37.78%) 34 (28.33%)	(62.22%) 56 (46.67%)	(100%) 90 (37.5%)
Buy from Stalls	(67.86%) 19 (15.83%)	(32.14%) 09 (7.5%)	(100%) 28 (11.67%)
Go Home for Tiffin	(20.83%) 05 (4.17%)	(79.17%) 19 (15.83%)	(100%) 24 (10%)
Total	(50%) 120 (100%)	(50%) 120 (100%)	(100%) 240 (100%)

Parents are usually supposed to teach the children to conduct themselves in such ways that they fit into the society. Parents expect their children to behave well. Though the common method of disciplining children in most households is to spank the child when s/he misbehaves. Many other methods are also in use. Some of them are found to be more effective than others. A few of the disciplinary methods that are common in a normal home are corporal punishment,

Table 6.12b: Distribution of sample students in terms of their age group and type of tiffin they take to school [N=240]

Type of Tiffin at School	*Age Group*			*Total*
	< 12 Yrs.	*13-14 Yrs.*	*>15 Yrs.*	
No Tiffin	(18.75%) 03 (4.17%)	(25%) 04 (4.35%)	(56.25%) 09 (11.84%)	(100%) 16 (6.67%)
Cooked Tiffin	(39.02%) 32 (44.44%)	(36.59%) 30 (32.61%)	(24.39%) 20 (26.32%)	(100%) 82 (34.17%)
Ready-made Tiffin	(34.44%) 31 (43.06%)	(46.67%) 42 (45.65%)	(18.89%) 17 (22.37%)	(100%) 90 (37.5%)
Buy from Stalls	(7.14%) 02 (2.78%)	(35.72%) 10 (10.87%)	(57.14%) 16 (21.05%)	(100%) 28 (11.67%)
Go Home for Tiffin	(16.67%) 04 (5.55%)	(25%) 06 (6.52%)	(58.33%) 14 (18.42%)	(100%) 24 (10%)
Total	(30%) 72 (100%)	(38.33%) 92 (100%)	(31.67%) 76 (100%)	(100%) 240 (100%)

advising the child by giving reasons, scolding and ignoring the child by withdrawing affection. Sternberg *et al.* (1993: 44) and Straus (1994: 76) explain that punishment is degrading, it contributes to feelings of helplessness and humiliation, robs a child of self-worth and self-respect, thus leading to withdrawal or aggression. Straus, Sugarman and Gilessimss (1997: 761) state that children who get spanked regularly are more likely overtime to cheat or lie and show less remorse for wrong doing. During the course of my interview a male student of class VI, studying in CSBZS states:

> "I often get scolded/beaten by my father for small mistakes. He is very strict by nature. His more presence in the house during my study hours creates fear within me. I never feel confident to disclose my wrong doings to him."

The above mentioned statement of Subrat reflects his impression on his father. Probably his father is not friendly to him; rather he keeps a distance with Subrat. Many a time Subrat is punished for the minor mistakes. He fears to admit his faults knowing the fact that his father will not spare him. He also avoids making any discussion with his father regarding his problems. It appears as if his father lacks understanding. This may adversely affect his mental make up.

Analysis in (Tables 6.13a,b,c) reveals that of the 240 sample students, 60 (25.00%) opined that they get heavy punishment at home by their parents, of which 80.00 per cent are male and the remaining 20.00 per cent are female. 96 (40.00%) of the students reported that they get moderate degree of punishment, of which one-third are male and two-third are female. The remaining 84 (35.00%) students felt

Table 6.13a: Distribution of sample students in terms of nature of punishment at home and sex [N=240]

Sex	*Nature of Punishment at Home*			*Total*
	Heavy	*Moderate*	*Light*	
Male	(40%) 48 (80%)	(26.67%) 32 (33.33%)	(33.33%) 40 (47.62%)	(100%) 120 (50%)
Female	(10%) 12 (20%)	(53.33%) 64 (66.67%)	(36.67%) 44 (52.38%)	(100%) 120 (50%)
Total	(25%) 60 (100%)	(40%) 96 (100%)	(35%) 84 (100%)	(100%) 240 (100%)

Table 6.13b: Distribution of sample students in terms of nature of punishment at home and age group [N=240]

Age Group	*Nature of Punishment at Home*			*Total*
	Heavy	*Moderate*	*Light*	
< 12 Yrs.	(30.56%) 22 (36.67%)	(38.89%) 28 (29.17%)	(30.56%) 22 (26.19%)	(100%) 72 (30%)
13-14 Yrs.	(9.78%) 09 (15%)	(51.09%) 47 (48.96%)	(39.13%) 36 (42.86%)	(100%) 92 (38.33%)
> 15 Yrs.	(38.16%) 29 (48.33%)	(27.63%) 21 (21.87%)	(34.21%) 26 (30.95%)	(100%) 76 (31.67%)
Total	(25%) 60 (100%)	(40%) 96 (100%)	(35%) 84 (100%)	(100%) 240 (100%)

Table 6.13c: Distribution of sample students in terms of nature of punishment at home and course affiliation [N=240]

Course Affiliation	*Nature of Punishment at Home*			*Total*
	Heavy	*Moderate*	*Light*	
	(23.75%)	(50%)	(26.25%)	(100%)
ICSE	19	40	21	80
	(31.67%)	(41.67%)	(25%)	(33.33%)
	(18.75%)	(46.25%)	(35%)	(100%)
CBSE	15	37	28	80
	(25%)	(38.54%)	(33.33%)	(33.33%)
	(32.5%)	(23.75%)	(43.75%)	(100%)
HSC	26	19	35	80
	(43.33%)	(19.79%)	(41.67%)	(33.34%)
	(25%)	(40%)	(35%)	(100%)
Total	60	96	84	240
	(100%)	(100%)	(100%)	(100%)

that light type of punishment is given to them by their parents, of which 47.62 per cent are male and 52.38 per cent are female.

In order to further assess the frequency of punishment given by their parents at home, data have been collected on the frequency of punishment. Of the 240 sample students, 62 (25.83%) are frequently punished by their parents at home, of which 59.68 per cent are of M.E. level students and 40.32 per cent are of high school level students. 108 (45.00%) of the students occasionally get punished by their parents, of which 42.59 per cent are at M.E. level and 57.41 per cent are at high school level. The remaining 70 (29.17%) students never get punished at home, of which 87.14 per cent are M.E. level students and 12.86 per cent are high school level students (Table 6.14a,b,c).

Table 6.14a: Distribution of sample students in terms of frequency of punishment at home and sex [N=240]

Sex	*Frequency of Punishment at Home*			*Total*
	Never	*Occasionally*	*Frequently*	
	(11.67%)	(49.17%)	(39.17%)	(100%)
Male	14	59	47	120
	(20%)	(54.63%)	(75.81%)	(50%)
	(46.67%)	(40.83%)	(12.5%)	(100%)
Female	56	49	15	120
	(80%)	(45.37%)	(24.19%)	(50%)
	(29.17%)	(45%)	(25.83%)	(100%)
Total	70	108	62	240
	(100%)	(100%)	(100%)	(100%)

Table 6.14b: Distribution of sample students in terms of frequency of punishment at home and age group [N=240]

Age Group	*Frequency of Punishment at Home*			*Total*
	Never	*Occasionally*	*Frequently*	
< 12 Yrs.	(11.11%) 08 (11.43%)	(47.22%) 34 (31.48%)	(41.67%) 30 (48.39%)	(100%) 72 (30%)
13-14 Yrs.	(38.04%) 35 (50%)	(41.3%) 38 (35.19%)	(20.65%) 19 (30.65%)	(100%) 92 (38.33%)
> 15 Yrs.	(35.53%) 27 (38.57%)	(47.37%) 36 (33.33%)	(17.1%) 13 (20.97%)	(100%) 76 (31.67%)
Total	(29.17%) 70 (100%)	(45%) 108 (100%)	(25.83%) 62 (100%)	(100%) 240 (100%)

Table 6. 14c: Distribution of sample students in terms of frequency of punishment at home and course affiliation [N=240]

Course Affiliation	*Frequency of Punishment at Home*			*Total*
	Never	*Occasionally*	*Frequently*	
ICSE	(31.25%) 25 (35.71%)	(40%) 32 (29.63%)	(28.75%) 23 (37.1%)	(100%) 80 (33.33%)
CBSE	(35%) 28 (40%)	(55%) 44 (40.74%)	(10%) 08 (12.9%)	(100%) 80 (33.33%)
HSC	(21.25%) 17 (24.29%)	(40%) 32 (29.63%)	(38.75%) 31 (50%)	(100%) 80 (33.34%)
Total	(29.17%) 70 (100%)	(45%) 108 (100%)	(25.83%) 62 (100%)	(100%) 240 (100%)

Parents always get angry for their child's mistakes. Parents are also under wrong impression that they must get angry or punish their child for his mistakes to get better result. Parenting is an art with proper composition of fear and love. To get recovered from any disease, prescribed dose should only to be taken, otherwise, in spite of getting cured it might prove to be fatal. Only love or only fear is a never a sensible act as a parent. So, parents must have to understand their child's psychology and act accordingly. It is essential for all-round development of child.

Traditionally in our society, children are viewed as the property of their parents. The very fact of their physical weakness, lack of knowledge and experience renders children dependent on the adults around them. Marginalization can be located to physical stages, to which children may not be permitted entrance, be that because of dangerous environments as children must be cared for while parents are doing something else. Childhood is marginalized in as much as children are always placed in the department for minors. They are marginalized from our system of remuneration and distribution in the sense that their activities are not thought of as having economic worth, or it is families, not children, who are targeted.

Affections are emotional reactions built up through pleasant associations. The affection the child develops for parents depend upon the type of relationship they have with him. Garrison (1982: 151) emphasized a constant rejection in the home may leave the child's capacity by giving forth affection undeveloped or may cause him to seek affection from individuals outside the home. As a child grows, his association with the parents changes. They always expect a friendly relationship with their parents. In this case, it is not ideal on the part of the parents to be very strict in imposing rules and regulations. Some parents are very strict regarding children's discipline and academic performance. They demand excessive exactness from their children, which the child fails to comply. They have also some reservation for higher technical education for girls.

In a similar vein, Jayashree's mother tells:

> "I am not in favour of providing very high level of education for girls. That is why I do not encourage my daughter to go for any technical education. After completing her class Xth examination, it is important for her to concentrate more on household activities which will finally help her to be a good housewife/mother-in-law/daughter-in-law."

The above statement highlights the negative attitude of some parents towards female education. Jayashree's mother feels that higher technical education for her daughter is meaningless. Those would be of no use after her marriage. Rather learning how to cook and other household activities will be of a great benefit to Jayshree in her in-law house. This type of thinking by Jayshree's mother may spoil her career.

Our study reflects the attitude of the parents towards their children. 36 (15.00%) students reported that their parents are very strict, of which one-forth are male and three-fourth are female. 63 (26.25%) students opined that their parents are somewhat strict, of which 46.03 per cent are male and 53.97 per cent are female. 45 (18.75%) students stated that their parents attitude towards them is neutral of which 31.11 per cent are male and 68.89 per cent are female. 52 (21.67%) students stated that their parents are somewhat liberal towards them, of which 61.54 per cent are male and 38.46 per cent are female. The remaining 44 (18.33%) told that their parents are very much liberal, of which 81.82 per cent are male and 18.18 per cent are female (Table 6.15a,b,c).

Table 6.15a: Distribution of sample students in terms of their sex and opinion on the attitude of parents [N=240]

Attitude of parents	*Sex*		*Total*
	Male	*Female*	
Very much strict	(25%) 09 (7.5%)	(75%) 27 (22.5%)	(100%) 36 (15%)
Somewhat strict	(46.06%) 29 (24.17%)	(53.97%) 34 (28.33%)	(100%) 63 (26.25%)
Neutral	(31.11%) 14 (11.69%)	(68.89%) 31 (25.83%)	(100%) 45 (18.75%)
Very much liberal	(81.82%) 36 (30%)	(18.18%) 08 (6.67%)	(100%) 44 (18.33%)
Somewhat liberal	(61.54%) 32 (26.67%)	(38.46%) 20 (16.67%)	(100%) 52 (21.67%)
Total	(50%) 120 (100%)	(50%) 120 (100%)	(100%) 240 (100%)

A female student of SJCHS, studying in class X narrates:

> "I have a great deal of interest in song and dance. But I am not allowed to attend coaching classes. My father is very strict as regard to my mobility. He dislikes my movement alone outside the house especially after sunset. I do not like this restrictions."

Table 6.15b: Distribution of sample students in terms of their age group and opinion on the attitude of parents [N=240]

Attitude of parents	*Age Group*			*Total*
	< 12 Yrs.	*13-14 Yrs.*	*>15 Yrs.*	
Very much strict	(2.78%) 01 (1.39%)	(55.55%) 20 (21.74%)	(41.67%) 15 (19.74%)	(100%) 36 (15%)
Somewhat strict	(22.22%) 14 (19.44%)	(50.79%) 32 (34.78%)	(26.99%) 17 (22.37%)	(100%) 63 (26.25%)
Neutral	(55.55%) 25 (34.72%)	(26.67%) 12 (13.04%)	(17.78%) 08 (10.52%)	(100%) 45 (18.75%)
Very much liberal	(40.91%) 18 (25%)	(13.64%) 06 (6.52%)	(45.45%) 20 (26.32%)	(100%) 44 (18.33%)
Somewhat liberal	(26.92%) 14 (19.44%)	(42.31%) 22 (23.91%)	(30.77%) 16 (21.05%)	(100%) 52 (21.67%)
Total	(30%) 72 (100%)	(38.33%) 92 (100%)	(31.67%) 76 (100%)	(100%) 240 (100%)

Table 6.15c: Distribution of sample students in terms of their course affiliation and opinion on the attitude of parents [N=240]

Attitude of parents	*Course Affiliation*			*Total*
	ICSE	*CBSE*	*HSC*	
Very much strict	(47.22%) 17 (21.25%)	(30.56%) 11 (13.75%)	(22.22%) 08 (10%)	(100%) 36 (15%)
Somewhat strict	(34.92%) 22 (27.5%)	(39.68%) 25 (31.25%)	(25.4%) 16 (20%)	(100%) 63 (26.25%)
Neutral	(22.22%) 10 (12.5%)	(40%) 18 (22.5%)	(37.78%) 17 (21.25%)	(100%) 45 (18.75%)
Very much liberal	(27.27%) 12 (15%)	(27.27%) 12 (15%)	(45.46%) 20 (25%)	(100%) 44 (18.33%)
Somewhat liberal	(36.54%) 19 (23.75%)	(26.92%) 14 (17.5%)	(36.54%) 19 (23.75%)	(100%) 52 (21.67%)
Total	(33.33%) 80 (100%)	(33.33%) 80 (100%)	(33.34%) 80 (100%)	(100%) 240 (100%)

The above statement by Firoza shows her personal feelings. It seems that her father is a strict disciplinarian. Though her family is custom bound by their traditions, but in recent times girls move out alone from their homes. We are now passing through a phase between subjugation and emancipation and have entered the outside world leaving behind the age-old tradition of domestic confinement. At times Firoza tries to convince her father but her father has other ideas. This creates a sort of relative deprivation within Firoza.

A grown up child dislikes remaining under restrictions. S/he expects freedom. One of our respondents stated that he stays in his uncle's house for perusing his studies. He does not like the threatening atmosphere in his uncle's house. He is prevented from doing many things. He is always expected to be around his study table, which becomes very difficult for him. This has created misunderstandings between him and his uncle and aunty several times (Case Study 9).

In those sample families where both the parents are working, the children are the worst sufferers. In such cases the parents fail to give adequate attention to the educational progress of their children. They feel tired after returning to home from their work place and thus left with a little energy to supervise their children's educational matters. In such a situation the child feels alienated. S/he no longer enjoys his/her study and thereby develops a sense of self-estrangement.

The time parents and children spend together is getting shorter. Breakfasts together are disappearing, as is, to some extent, dinner around the family table. It is a place where the experiences of the day are shared, and the family history and personal biographies are constructed and reconstructed in a very significant way. Children walks and hikes with parents take up less than an hour a week. Not just work but family life needs time, time filled meaningfully for both parents and children. The chronic lack of time on the part of adults, briefly expressed in the familiar and current statement – "Wait, I have no time just now", marks an area of potential psychological sub-deprivation in many apparently well-functioning families.

In our study where both parents are working, the children are seen feeling isolated and neglected. Their parents are so busy throughout the day that they hardly get time to share with the children. Their parents cannot make themselves practically involved with the children. In some families it is observed that a maidservant is deputed to look after the children. In this cases the children lack parental love and affection. It is marked that after performing their duties, the parents come back home carrying many office work. Some parents, who are teachers, take tuition classes in their home after returning from school. Getting exhausted at the end of the day, they feel irritated on their children even for a slightest mistake. Such a situation in the home creates mental tension for the children.

In cases where both the parents are employed or where only mothers are employed, children are highly neglected. They lack proper supervision and guidance. Besides that in such cases the workload on the girl-child increases, as she has to do additional household works in the absence of her mother. She has to take care of the younger siblings (if any) during that period (Case Study 10).

A female student of class VII, studying in MCPS says:

> "Both my parents are working, so they do not have enough time to keep track of my educational progress. Occasionally my mummy assists me in my studies. She is so busy in the working days that she hardly gets time to talk to me."

Snigdha's statement indicates the busy schedule of her parents. It appears that she gets very less assistance from her parents in her studies. Her father goes to his job place early in the morning and returns late in the night. At time Snigdha does not meet her father even once in a day. She feels jealous when she sees her friends with their parents. This makes her to feel uncared and neglected.

The most painful loneliness is not when one is alone, but when one is in the presence of others and yet feel separated, excluded and cut off from the shared world of the others. The desire to belong to the others' shared world – the world outside oneself – is frustrated by the impossibility of achieving this. It creates a vacuum between these children and the others and inside themselves. This reveals the feelings of being excluded, unwanted and disliked (Kirova–Petrova, 2000: 108). The quality and quantity of the time spend together by parents and children are very important. The imbalance between work and leisure, combined with a feeling of being exceedingly pressed for time leads to having insufficient sleep and a disrupted sleep rhythm, particularly among employed mothers. Psychological time is thus, often devalued. As a result the devastating environment is often accompanied by a threatening deterioration in the relationship with the child, which especially jeopardizes children's well-being (Graph 10).

Graph 10: Distribution of sample students in terms of their course affiliation and working status of their parents [N=240]

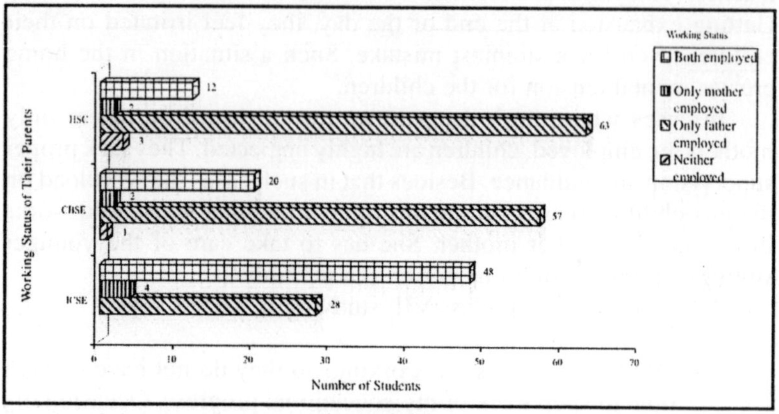

What follows here is a remark by one of the parents of a respondent:

> "Both of us are working in Government organizations. Sheela's mother returns home at 4.30 pm. I come back from office late in the evening, as I am holding a key position in my office. We feel very tired and exhausted by the time we come back from our work place. We fail to give more time to Sheela to assist her in her studies. Just a week before the examinations my wife takes leave from her office to help Sheela in her studies."

This experience reflects the situation of a family where the children feel alienated. It shows that they are somewhat cut off from the shared world. The assistance and encouragement that should have been given to Sheela by her mother throughout the year got condensed to only a week. However, her father has even no time for Sheela as he feels his office work more important than Sheela's educational progress. Sheela is slowly getting used to her father's unconcerned attitude towards her. She rather says "my father is a busy person and therefore, he fails to give me more time."

Table 6.16a,b,c represents the working status of parents of our sample students. In case of 80 (33.33%) students both parents are employed[6], of which 60.00 per cent are from ICSE background, 25.00

Table 6.16a: Distribution of sample students in terms of their sex and working status of the parents [N=240]

Working status of parents	*Sex*		*Total*
	Male	*Female*	
Neither employed	(75%) 03 (2.5%)	(25%) 01 (0.83%)	(100%) 04 (1.67%)
Only father employed	(62.84%) 93 (77.5%)	(37.16%) 55 (45.83%)	(100%) 148 (61.67%)
Only mother employed	(37.5%) 03 (2.5%)	(62.5%) 05 (4.17%)	(100%) 08 (3.33%)
Both employed	(26.25%) 21 (17.5%)	(73.75%) 59 (49.17%)	(100%) 80 (33.33%)
Total	(50%) 120 (100%)	(50%) 120 (100%)	(100%) 240 (100%)

Table 6.16b: Distribution of sample students in terms of their age group and working status of the parents [N=240]

Working status of parents	*Age Group*			*Total*
	< 12 Yrs.	*13-14 Yrs.*	*>15 Yrs.*	
Neither employed	(75%) 03 (4.17%)	(25%) 01 (1.09%)	— (1.67%)	(100%) 04
Only father employed	(33.78%) 50 (69.44%)	(41.89%) 62 (67.39%)	(24.33%) 36 (47.37%)	(100%) 148 (61.67%)
Only mother employed	(50%) 04 (5.56%)	(25%) 02 (2.17%)	(25%) 02 (2.63%)	(100%) 08 (3.32%)
Both employed	(18.75%) 15 (20.83%)	(33.75%) 27 (29.35%)	(47.5%) 38 (50%)	(100%) 80 (33.33%)
Total	(30%) 72 (100%)	(38.33%) 92 (100%)	(31.67%) 76 (100%)	(100%) 240 (100%)

Table 6.16c: Distribution of sample students in terms of their course affiliation and working status of the parents [N=240]

Working status of parents	*Course Affiliation*			*Total*
	ICSE	*CBSE*	*HSC*	
Neither employed	—	(25%) 01 (1.25%)	(75%) 03 (3.75%)	(100%) 04 (1.67%)
Only father employed	(18.92%) 28 (35%)	(38.51%) 57 (71.25%)	(42.57%) 63 (78.75%)	(100%) 148 (61.67%)
Only mother employed	(50%) 04 (5%)	(25%) 02 (2.5%)	(25%) 02 (2.5%)	(100%) 08 (3.32%)
Both employed	(60%) 48 (60%)	(25%) 20 (25%)	(15%) 12 (15%)	(100%) 80 (33.33%)
Total	(33.33%) 80 (100%)	(33.33%) 80 (100%)	(33.34%) 80 (100%)	(100%) 240 (100%)

per cent are from CBSE background and the remaining 15.00 per cent are from HSC background. 8 (3.33%) students have only their mothers employed, of which 50.00 per cent belong to ICSE background, one-fourth are from CBSE background and another one-fourth are from HSC background. 148 (61.67%) students have only their fathers employed, of which 18.92 per cent are from ICSE background, 38.51 per cent are from CBSE course and 42.57 per cent are from HSC course. The remaining 4 (1.67%) students have neither their father nor mother employed, of which 25.00 per cent are from CBSE background and 75.00 per cent are from HSC background.

A characteristic feature of modern childhood is the handing over to women of the emotional, practical and economic responsibility for children. It is a feature that is brought to the extreme in the emerging mother-child family. It is claimed that there is a worldwide increase in the number of children living with single mothers. As resources have been drawn from the family through the mother's employment, little compensation has been forthcoming from societal sources. This represents feminization of childhood. Tragically, it is still unrecognized that childhood represents an important and constructive part of the social fabric of any society.

Today competition is a part of life. Every parent wishes as his child to be winner in this competition. While parents try for that only, they do not think of child's mental capacity or interest. It makes the child frustrate and helpless. Instead of getting encourgement to stand firmly in this compititive world, the children find out the way of commiting suicide. If parents do not think that their child should not choose the path of disaster, they only must try to cultivate an open hearted approach to their child and keep all the views transparent. Knowledge should flourish like flowers. Any forcible attempt, in order to achieve the target, may mistrack them and parents may loose them forever.

NOTES

1. When I tell that they do not have a study room, I mean that they do not have a separate room for studying. The room in which they study is also used by members of the family for other purposes.
2. A symbolic term for the society of Internet "Citizens".
3. Citizen of the Internet (from Net and Citizen).
4. It is an institution of the Christian community where moral teachings are given from the Bible. The division of the students into different classes is done on the basis of age group. The prescribed course remains the same in all the Sunday schools in the State.
5. Holiday homework is given to keep the students in touch with the studies throughout the vacation with an idea that they make proper utilization of the time.
6. By employed I mean those parents who are primarily engaged either in government or non-government organizations for earning their livelihood.

7

Conclusion

Childhood is a cultural construction and very much a part and parcel of our complex social order. It refers to a phase of life and a category of human beings defined as "children". Childhood is universally recognized as a period when the child is helpless, defenseless and dependent on adults, especially the parents, for his/her well-being. Parents and society are expected to serve the child unconditionally to develop his/her potential and groom him/her to assume the responsibilities of adulthood. However, it is a matter of serious concern that children are not even given due scope to voice their views in matters affecting their own lives.

Modern childhood constructs children out of society, mutes their voices and denies their personhood (Alanen, 1990; Ennew, 1991; Oldman, 1994; Mayall, 1994; Qvortrup, 1994). Childhood as a social construction belongs to nobody, but everybody competes with everybody else to control it. The possible competitors are the society/school, the family and children themselves. "Children who in every society are by definition excluded from power game, control the childhood the least" (Shamgar-Handelman, 1994: 264).

Countless children in our contemporary society have advanced almost directly from infancy into adulthood and if they ever experienced childhood, it is only a fleeting stage. The adult conspiracies against childhood thrive. The quality of childhood has clearly deteriorated. Children of contemporary society are overburdened. Children are thus excluded from adult world. Mehta (2001: 263) states that the society has a special obligation towards children, whose lack of maturity and means, whose vulnerability and dependence bring in the family and community to protect the children from external as well internal dangers fulfilling all the required needs. An all-round effort needs to be made from the micro to macro levels in family, school and community to protect child "rights". Throughout our study we have tried to highlight the disappearance of childhood. We share the views of Qvortrup that "childhood is a permanent form, even if its members change continuously and even if it is itself at historically at variance" (Qvortrup, 1994: 23).

The present work is a humble attempt to study the school-going children of Sambalpur city. Of the 18 High Schools in the city, only four are selected as the sample schools. They are: St. Joseph's Convent High School, Madnabati Central Public School, Chandra Sekhar Behera Zilla School and Municipal Girls' High School. The students of the sample schools are exposed to three different types of course curriculum: ICSE, CBSE and HSC. Students from class VI to class X have been covered in this study. All the sample students are between less than 12 and more than 15 years of age. Data are collected from 240 sample students by random sampling method. Information has been gathered with the help of interview, observation and case study methods.

The school is not only about learning facts and figures. The UN Convention on the Rights of the Child expresses views about the spirit in the school and the values to be taught. Education should aim at developing the child's personality, talents and mental and physical abilities to the fuller potential. It should prepare the child for a responsible life in a free society, in the spirit of understanding, peace, tolerance, equality of sexes and friendship among the people. Respect for human rights is mentioned specifically in Article 29. Article 31 covers the right of the child to rest, leisure and play. The present day competitive and expanding school system contributes heavily to the development of an educational ideology of upbringing. School has further institutionalized the separation of the children from the society, confirming upon them a separate identity: their proper place is in the classroom.

School does not mean just education and school work. The most important factor for many children, at least for some time, is that school is first of all the place where peers meet, friendships are made and some fun is experienced. It is a place to learn not just from adults but also from their own kind, people of their own age or those who are only a little older (Kovaqik, 1994: 113). The teacher should provide each individual student equal opportunity to find growth and fulfilment along directions most suited to his individual abilities and interests.

Unless the syllabus of every subject is, on the one hand, lightened by dropping uninteresting and useless subject matters and on the other hand, enriched by the inclusion of interesting and significant materials that will give joy and insight to students, it will not become a truly educative medium. The sample students are exposed to too-extensive textbooks, excessively complex subject matter, unintelligible formulations, a host of scientific terms, abstract concepts, encyclopaedic facts in textbooks, etc. There has been the inclusion of many diversified courses of study into the present syllabus.

Results of the study reveal that most of the sample students face difficulty in some specific subjects as they find the course to be very vast. Our analysis shows that the ICSE course is more difficult as compared to the CBSE and HSC course curriculum. It is significant to mention that most of the teachers of the sample schools follow non-participatory method of teaching. A "monologue classroom situation" is a common sight. Of the total number of 240 sample students, 72.50 per cent attend coaching classes. Many students even attend two tuition classes in a day. It is interesting to note that many teachers deliberately do not teach well in the school, which forces the students to attend tuition classes for extra-coaching in those subjects. Going to school and then attending the coaching classes in a single day is quite tiring for school students.

Our findings further show that teachers always have sky-high expectation from the students and the students find it really difficult to attain that level. Apart from a good academic performance, the teachers always expect that the students should participate in the extra-curricular activities of the school like: annual function, *pujas,* science exhibition, games and sports, etc. Our data reveal that maximum students participate in the sports conducted by the school. Teachers often foment competition and competitive thinking assuming that such an approach leads to success. 60.83 per cent of the students in our study opined that their class-teachers are non-cooperative by nature. Various techniques are employed by the teachers to discipline the students. The students do not feel emotionally secure. Repeated punishment has made some of them stubborn.

It is the school that determines how much time remains with the child. The school intrudes into family life by means of homework, which often requires the assistance of parents. Our analysis reflects that maximum students, *i.e.* 40.83 per cent opined that the volume of homework is heavy. It is observed that homework is given to the students in every subject. It becomes difficult for a student to complete both the school and tuition homework.

Results point out that unrelenting competitiveness is destructive not only in the classroom but right through life. Many great teachers have been concerned about the aspect of fear and anxiety engendered by competition in the classroom. The highest function of the education is not only to bring about academic excellence, but more important, the psychological freedom of the student himself. Competition exists only when there is comparison, and comparison does not bring about excellence. Being constantly pitted against one another, children can hardly develop excellence of spirit. Excessive competition in examinations has led to anguish among students.

Parents must maintain a healthy attitude and affectionate behaviour towards their children. It is seen that 88.33 per cent of the students reported that their parents are much concerned about them. Parents usually hold high aspiration about their children's academic performance. Apart from academics, parents are also concerned about the socialization and the development of personality of the child. Mead (1930: 320) made a study of educational and socialization processes of Manus of New Guniea. She dealt with the enculturation processes by which they brought their children up form infancy to childhood and childhood to adulthood. She deals with educative role of culture in development of personality of a child through different ages of life such as infancy, childhood and adulthood. The child keeps up to their expectations because he has high regard for them and their attitudes. However, unlike the New Guniea case the children in our complex order are brought up in quite a different environment where fast learning and competitiveness are highly valued.

As a child grows, his/her association with the parents changes. S/he always expects a friendly attitude from the parents. In such a case, it is not ideal on the part of the parents to be very strict in imposing rules and regulations on the children. Our analysis shows that 15.00 per cent parents are very strict regarding discipline and academic performance of their children. 25.00 per cent of the children reported that they receive heavy punishment from their parents at home. This type of attitude from the parents makes the children feel depressed. Parents always demand excessive exactness from their children, which the latter fail to comply.

As a matter of fact, when the child grows up, the parents expect him/her to shoulder up some of the burdens of the home. Thus, the child gets burdened with domestic work. Our study shows that most of the female students of higher age group assist their mothers in the household activities like cleaning utensils, sweeping, assisting in cooking, taking care of younger siblings, etc. Some boys are also seen doing some non-domestic work like fetching portable water/milk and marketing.

In spite of the busy schedule, the sample students maintain some study hours at home. In order to have a congenial study environment, a study room is essential. This gives an opportunity to a child to concentrate in the study. However, as many as 60.83 per cent of the sample students do not have a separate study room. The space used by them during their study hours is also simultaneously used by other family members for performing their routine activities. In some families it is seen that there is always a rush of guest in the house, which disturbs the study environment of the child. Our data reveal that only 39.17 per cent of the students have a separate study room. As many as 67.50 per cent of the students reported that a non-congenial atmosphere prevails in their houses.

Apart from studying the course curriculum, the sample students are seen taking extra-coaching in various fields, viz. song, dance, computers, karatte, yoga and typing. Parents expect that their children should gain super-excellence in different fields including studies. As many as 34.17 per cent of the sample students are found admitted in computer institutions, whereas 28.33 per cent students take coaching in song and dance. Though it is good to learn something extra but it increases the workload of the already overburdened child. It appears to be impossible for a school student at this tender age to bear such a burden. Thus children find it really difficult to combine their studies, tuitions, homework and the extra-coaching simultaneously and successfully.

School children enjoy themselves the most during the vacations. It is a period of relaxation after a long time of pressure from school studies, tuitions, extra-coaching, etc. However, it is found that some of our sample children are not even spared from academic activities during the vacations. They are assigned with heavy holiday homework by their teachers. 28.33 per cent of the students opined that they spend maximum time in doing holiday homework during the vacation. Sunday is a holiday when the school children are free from the routine activities. They spend their time in various activities like: watching T.V., playing, reading magazines/story books, etc. But it is observed that 24.17 per cent of the students spend maximum time in studies on Sundays. During the week days, the students are seen watching television during leisure hours. Maximum students, i.e. 38.75 per cent watch television for 1 to 2 hours a day.

Parents with better educational background will be able to give better guidance to their children. Our study shows that either of the parent or in some cases both the parents assist the sample students in their studies when they are back at home. In those families where both the parents are working, the children are the worst sufferers. In such cases the parents fail to give adequate attention to the educational progress of the children. In our study 33.33 per cent of the students have both their parents employed. Here•the parents feel tired after returning home from the work place. The time parents and children spend together is short. In such a situation the children feel alienated. They lack proper supervision and guidance. The quality and quantity of time spent together by parents and children is very important. The chronic lack of time on the part of the adults, briefly expressed in the familiar and current statement – "Wait, I have no time just now".

Pedagogic methods have to be devised where a feeling of competitiveness is not the dominant spur to achievement. One can safely assert that if a child is brought up in a non-competitive ambience, he is more likely to succeed even in the competitive world outside. The fear of not reaching the top rank of the ladder does not crush him emotionally. Therefore, he tends to be more successful. If he succeeds, he takes it in his stride, with a wholesome understanding of other aspirants. He does not let the anguish of comparison and competition eat into his bone marrow. Striving competitively becomes a way of thinking and leads to heavier burden on the mind with the passing of years. Understanding and acceptance of varying talents in oneself and others should be cultivated. Co-operation with others will make for harmony within the self and in relationship with others.

It is important to recognize that our perceptions of childhood undergo constant changes and are in many ways ambivalent and contradictory. For many adults, childhood is imbued with a rather romanticized notion of innocence – a period free from responsibility or conflict and dominated by fantasy, play and opportunity. Yet for many children from different cultures and classes the dominating feature of childhood is that of powerlessness and lack of control over what happens to them. Some adults perceive children as essentially irrational, irresponsible and incapable of making choices on matters of concern to them and to a large extent our legislation still reflects this view.

Clearly the degree of vulnerability diminishes rapidly as they grow older and become more able to exercise responsibility for themselves. Children are vulnerable because of their complete lack of political and economic power and their lack of civil rights in our society. This aspect of childhood derives from historical attitudes and presumptions about the nature of childhood. Children spend a considerable portion of their existence at school. School, as a socialization instrument is, therefore, expected to be an adequate reflection of development in society despite the strong demands of the human rights project and the binding provisions in its reflecting human rights instruments.

It is very surprising that our sample schools are clearly shirking their responsibilities. For the best, occasionally some faculties are dealing with this basic issue. No intentional and systematic comprehensive programme is set up until now. The principle that children have equal rights as human beings is not given the primary consideration. The school does not give due weightage to the child's opinion. It probably fails to recognize that each child has rights that are of great importance. The "rights of children" is an abstract, general and legalistic concept. It does not help children until it is put into practice. Rights without services are meaningless (Gross and Gross, 1977: 6).

Children change with every generation in terms of intellectual and cultural, rather than physical development. But the harsh conditions, in which the majority of them live, place them in the very heart of the social problems which contribute to their earlier transition into maturity, and is some cases faster ageing. The moment has come that we see them not just as objects, but as subjects of their own life, education and development. Now when we decide what is good for the school-going children we should ask whether they share our opinion, consider their concept of good and evil, their interests, expectations and views. In short, we should accept the fact that they have rights and give them guarantees and the chance to exercise them.

The real crux of the matter is whether parents and teachers are willing to involve the children in decision-making concerning matters affecting their lives. How are the school-going students' own experiences and responses to policies directed towards them? Why should the students of Indian schools be exposed to an educational system that was devised 100 years ago in Victorian Colonial time and is thoroughly authoritarian? The teachers at school and parents at home force the child to concentrate in academics under the plea that they are doing it in the "best interest of the child". Though they work hard both at school and home, still their labour goes unrecognized. Children should not be placed under pressure cooker to achieve mental excellence. Pushing them to grow up fastei intellectually, socially and psychologically will cripple them in their development and rob them of their childhood.

A few days ago a special report was telecast on Star News that "three school going students of Andhra Pradesh committed suicide". For this horrible incident the teachers and the parents of these students were held to be responsible. Because, those students were enforced upon expectation which was beyond their limits. Finally, being frustrated from life they decided to end their lives. These children were often overburdened with the hard work and mentally tortured by their parents and teachers. Even, the child psychology or mental approach of children never tried to understand these children. This unfortunate incident may get repeated anywhere, if the parents fail to act judiciously. The time is high to reduce the burden of the overburdened children.

Case Studies

Case Study 1

"A" is a stout, dark-complexioned, ordinary looking male student of class VI, of Madnabati Central Public School. He has two brothers and one sister. His father is a clerk and his mother is a housewife. "A" lives in a joint family of traditional lower-middle class.

"A" gets up early in the morning, as he has to attend a tuition class before going to school. After returning from the tuition, he hurriedly makes himself ready to leave for school. He stays at a distance of 2 km from the school. He goes to school by foot. "A" carries a heavy load of the school bag at his back. The school bag is tightly packed with the textbooks and notebooks of all the eight periods. In addition to this he carries a tiffin-box and a water bottle. The revised course curriculum has added to the thickness of the textbooks. This has thereby increased the weight of the school bag. The inclusion of the project work and the practical papers has over-loaded his shoulders. He feels tired by carrying this heavy load. After returning from school, "A" takes some light tiffin and goes out to play for an hour or so with his friends. In the evening a tutor comes to his house for coaching. Due to mental fatigue he often remains unmindful when his tutor teaches him. Having his dinner around 9.30 pm, he again read up to 11.30 pm for completing his homework. One of his brother is in the habit of reading loudly. As he reads along with his brothers and sister in one room, he fails to concentrate.

The two brothers sometimes have heated exchange on this matter. A's brother complain is that he remembers a lesson only when he reads it loudly. A's expectation to have a calm and quite study atmosphere is just not possible in a small house shared by six members. When he sees any of his brother/sister retiring to bed after the dinner, he also feels like sleeping. Being overburdened, he feels disgusted. Slowly he is loosing his interest in some difficult papers.

It becomes quite strenuous on the part of "A" to attend the coaching class in the morning and then going to school. Covering such long distance daily by walking is quite tiring for him.

Case Study 2

"B" is a slim, boy with average look. He is a student of Chandra Sekhar Behera Zilla School. He has a sister and two brothers. His father is a high school teacher. His mother is a staff nurse in the Government Hospital. "B" has failed in class VIII last year and is repeating the same class this year. He belongs to a well-to-do educated family.

"B" is a good sportsman. He always participates in the Annual Athletic Meet of the school. He plays both in-door and out-door games. He is a very good cricket player. He has won many prizes and medals in the inter-school cricket match. In the recess period and game period he is seen in the playground. After returning from school, he hurriedly changes his dress (uniform), takes some light tiffin and goes out to play with his friends.

His teachers encourage him to participate in the games and sports of the school, so as to earn good name and fame of the school. His interest in the school is not only confined to games and sports, but also in other extra-curricular activities like NCC and Red Cross. Apart from this, he also takes some coaching in karatte and attends computer classes. After returning from the playground he goes to attend karatte or computer classes. "B" spends most of his time in activities other then his studies. As a result, he fails to complete his school homework regularly.

His parents are displeased on him because of his over-involvement in games and sports. His failure in the previous examination was a big shock to his parents. This year they expect good performance from him in the examinations. They have tried their best to convince him, so that he concentrates more in his studies. At present they have engaged a good tutor who comes to their house daily and teaches him for 2 hours. Now "B" is trying to maintain some study hours. He now finds it difficult to concentrate both in his sporting activities and studies. He feels pressurized. This situation has made him more mentally unstable.

Case Study 3

"C" is a well-built student of class VIII of Chandra Sekhar Behera Zilla School. By nature he is out spoken with pleasing dispositions. He has one brother and four sisters. His father is a peon and his mother is a housewife. He belongs to an orthodox family with low economic background.

Though "C" is financially not very sound yet he takes interest in his studies. Both his parents have low level of educational standard. They do not understand the importance of education. "C" does not get any assistance in his studies from either of his parents or any family members. In the school his teachers are not very co-operative with him. As he is shy by nature, his classmates also maintain distance from him. As a result he does not receive any help from either his teachers or his friends.

His parents cannot afford to send him to any coaching class. They are not even in a position to provide him all the textbooks required for his studies. "C" does not play in the school during the recess time and in the game periods. During these periods he goes to the library and reads there. Books of the library are not allowed to be taken to home. He issues some books and prepares notes in the library itself. In spite of the indifferent attitude of the teachers and his friends he struggles hard to study. This results in more mental tension.

"C" utilizes his leisure in the school inside the library. Though he does not attend any coaching class or get any assistance at studies by his parents yet he has a good academic record. His performance in the school is good, but it would still be better if his parents could bestow more care and attention on him. His sole problem appears to be the confrontative and un-cooperative attitude of his teachers and friends. His personal efficiency, ability to work hard and tolerance have helped him to achieve success in studies.

Case Study 4

"D" is studying in class X of St. Joseph's Convent High School. He has only one brother. His general behaviour is not very pleasing. His father is a businessman and his mother is a housewife. He belongs to a well-to-do family.

Every working day "D" goes to school at 6.45 am. After returning from school he goes to attend computer classes. He spends much of his time in their shop during the evening hours. He assists his father in their family business. When his father remains out of station, he looks after the business. He is not much concerned with his studies. He does major part of the marketing for his family. He hardly gets time to study. His aim of life is to be a successful businessman. Therefore, he tries to make himself involved in their business. He is learning various market policies and strategies from his father.

All these engagements have diverted his mind from studies. He is regularly irregular in performing homework. Most of the time he remains punctual to the school timings. His class-teacher is displeased with such type of activities. He remains unmindful in the classroom. "D" is frequently punished by his teachers in the school. Repeated punishment has made him stubborn. He is disobedient, mischievous and moody. He had a poor performance in the previous examination.

It appears that he has got himself admitted to the school just to pass out the examination. Now he has to appear the final examination of class X. It is now increasingly difficult for him to concentrate on business and his studies at the same time. He does not feel confident to appear at the examination. Therefore, he is mentally a bit upset. Throughout the year he remained busy in other activities. Realizing the fact that the examination is fast approaching, he has now joined a coaching centre expecting to have a better performance.

Case Study 5

"E" is of a medium-statured, ordinary looking bulky girl. She is studying in class VIII of Madnabati Central Public School. Her father works in the Town Planning Office and her mother is a housewife. Her mother has paralysis and therefore fails to perform any work either for the family or for herself. She is bed-ridden. It all happened a couple of years ago when her mother had a heart stroke. "E" has a brother and a sister. As a member of a middle class family, "E" has been brought up in a traditional way.

She gets up early in the morning and prepares breakfast for all the family members. She then serves it to all and feeds separately her mother. She then prepares lunch and serves it to her brother and sister before going to school. They have a part-time maidservant who comes daily both in the morning and afternoon for cleaning the utensils, washing the clothes and sweeping the house. "E" hurriedly packs up the tiffin-box for herself and for her brother and sister and then leaves for school. In the recess period she comes home to feed her mother and to give her medicine, as her school is close by to her home. She quickly completes her duty and goes back to school. After returning from school she prepares tiffin for all the family members.

She does not get time to play with her friends. In the evening she looks after the studies of her younger brother and sister. She then completes her school homework and revises her courses. At times her father assists her in her studies. She has no time to attend any coaching class. "E" continues her study till late in the night. Sometimes her younger sister helps her in preparing dinner. She is very much occupied with the household works and in attending her mother. She feels very tired by the time she retires to bed. But she accepts life as it comes. She hardly receives assistance from anyone at home. She is unable to take proper care of her health.

"E" is an average student. Her feelings of anxiety and worry for home is very high. In spite of her familial obligations, she performs various types of household activities. She remains indecisive about her future studies. The domestic burden has forced her to develop such an attitude. This non-ending family problem has made her more housebound. She feels disheartened and helpless.

Case Study 6

"F" is a 14 years old boy with good facial features and pleasing manners. He has a brother and a sister. They are junior to him. His father is a lecturer and has recently been transferred to a college in Bhubaneswar. His mother is a school teacher. They maintain a higher standard of living. They stay in a rented house.

He goes to attend a coaching class in the morning hours. After returning he quickly gets himself ready for the school. After returning from school, he fetches milk by covering one and half kilometres. Some of the days he does marketing, especially when his father remains out of headquarters. He does not get enough time to play with his friends. He is a big support to his mother in the absence of his father. In the evening he goes to attend another tuition class. He gets completely exhausted by the time he returns home. He then assists his younger brother and sister in their studies. His mother does not get time to look after their studies. His mother remains busy throughout the day, as she has to do the household chores after returning from her school. The rest of her time is occupied in taking coaching classes of the students in her school.

The rush of guests to his house makes the home environment noisy in the evening hours. He does not have a separate study room. The room in which he studies is used by other members in the family. Therefore, he does not get a calm and peaceful study atmosphere in his house. Despite this limitation, he tries to complete both his school and tuition assignments. He reads late in the night to revises his courses. Sometime, he is found studying in the school during the game period. He sleeps for less than six hours in a day.

"F" is an intelligent student. He does not loose his calm due to frequent interruptions in his studies for one or the other reason. He feels ambivalent regarding his academic career.

Case Study 7

"G" is a short girl with a smiling face. She is studying in class VI of Municipal Girls' High School. As she is suffering from Polio, she uses two crutches for walking. She is the only child of her parents. Her father died when she was only two years old due to excessive drinking. Her mother sells vegetables in the Gole Bazar daily market. They also depend upon their grandparents and maternal uncle.

She became a victim to the deadly disease polio during her childhood due to the negligence of her parents. She was not immunized with triple antigen soon after her birth. She was attacked by polio when she was 4+. Physically she is not sound. She has been suffering from various diseases due to her poor resistance power.

Although "G" does not go to school regularly, she is a good student. She does not attend any coaching class due to their poor financial condition. Her school teachers are very co-operative with her. She is liked by all her friends and teachers because she is a good natured girl. All have a soft corner for her. One of her teacher comes to her house and guides her in studies. Though she is unable to go to school daily, she works hard at home for her studies. She invariably scores good marks in the examinations. She has a desire for higher studies.

G's mother is very much worried about her daughter's health. Her daughter is incapable to stand properly. She remains depressed thinking that no one will marry her physically handicapped daughter. She recounts that *"Lengdi tukel ke kie biha heba?"* (Who will marry this handicapped girl?). In spite of her physical disability she tries to do her own work by herself. She feels somewhat inferior when she compares herself with other students in her class. This creates a sort of relative deprivation in her mind.

Case Study 8

"H" is a thin good-looking girl. She is a student of class IX of Municipal Girls' High School. She stays in a small filthy house. Her father is a driver in the State Transport Department. Her mother died when she was 10 years old. Her father then got married to another wife. The economic condition of the family is not sound.

"H" has now a stepbrother. Her stepmother has a negative attitude towards her. She always asks "H" to assist her in the household works. "H" also takes care of her younger brother. Her stepmother goes on telling her father that a female child is a temporary member in a house. It is unwise to spend money on girl's education. He hardly finds time to read her lessons. She had a poor performance in the previous examination. She feels tired and frustrated due to heavy workload at home.

She does not get love and affection from her stepmother. She feels neglected and uncared in the family. Her brother is given more importance. He is given more quantity and nutritious food as compared to her. Some light tiffin is prepared for her father and brother in the evening. However, she is not given the evening tiffin. The food prepared for breakfast, lunch and dinner are mostly according to the choices of her brother and father. Her stepmother does not give her tiffin on a regular basis for the school.

Her father is also no more giving her the same attention. She does not get any assistance in her studies at home. She is even not sent out for any coaching class. "H" is not good at Mathematics, Science and English. She was detained last year in standard VIII because of her poor performance. She feels that she is discriminated in every field. She is forced to compromise with the compelling situation.

Case Study 9

"J" is a tall and smart boy studying in class VII of St. Joseph's Convent High School. He has only one sister. His father lives in a village and is primarily an agriculturalist. His mother is a housewife. As there are no educational facilities in his village, "J" has been staying in his uncle's house in Sambalpur for his studies for a couple of years.

He does not like the threatening atmosphere at his uncle's home. His aunty always exercises an authoritarian voice over him. They are very strict regarding his movement outside the house. He only gets opportunity to play with his friends in the school during the break. For a slightest mistake his uncle heavily punishes him. He does not attend any coaching class due to his poor economic condition. He prepares and revises his courses by himself. Sometimes his uncle assists him in his studies. As a grown up child, he dislikes to remain under so much restrictions. He expects more freedom from his uncle and aunty.

"J" is not permitted to watch television for more than ½ hour in a day. His aunty gets displeased when he watches programmes other than news and a selected serial. She always expects that "J" should be on the study table. Too much of study without play and recreation makes his mind dull. "J" keeps on counting days for the commencement of vacation so as to enable him to go to his home for meeting parents.

He is slowly losing his interest to continue his studies in Sambalpur. He is mentally suppressed. Though "J" has a good academic record, yet he is now in a state of confusion. He finds it difficult to adjust with his uncle and aunty. Sometime he finds the situation unbearable. There are many occasions of misunderstanding due to difference of opinion. He feels that it will be very difficult in his part to convince his parents regarding this matter. Much against his wishes, he continues to stay in his uncle's house leading somewhat an uncomfortable life.

Case Study 10

"K" is a tall fair-complexioned girl with average facial features. She is a student of class IX in Municipal Girls' High School. She has four brothers and a younger sister. Her father works in a bank and her mother is a school teacher. She is brought up in a large-sized middle class family. She is the eldest child in the family. When her parents leave the house for their duty, all the burdens of the family fall on her.

Early in the morning "K" gets up and goes to tuition. After returning from tuition, she assists her mother in cooking. The meals are prepared before 10.00 am as all the family members have to go to their respective job place/school. When she comes back from school, she sweeps the house, cleans the utensils and prepares tiffin. Her mother feels tired after returning from school. She serves tiffin to her younger brothers and sisters. "K" has to attend a lot of domestic chores. However she manages the house to everybody's satisfaction. She hardly gets time to play with her friends. Most of her time gets consumed by assisting her mother in the home. She admits that she fails to combine successfully her duties both a school and at home.

She does not get any leisure in a working day. In the evening she does her school and tuition homework. She also tries to revise her courses. After 8.00 p.m. she is found in the kitchen preparing dinner, as her mother takes some coaching classes of her school students in the evening. At times she is unable to complete the home assignments given by her teachers at school. But no one cares to realize her problems. In the midst of these situations she tries to find out time to help her younger brothers and sisters in their studies. In spite of the difficulties in carrying out her dual roles, she performs reasonably well in the examinations.

At an age of only 14 years "K" shoulders up a lot of responsibilities at home. Although "K" is hard working sometimes she loses her patience and gets irritated. She feels that no one is concerned with her educational progress. She thinks that she is neglected and uncared. She tries her best to perform better in the examinations.

Bibliography

Ahhunawallia, L.A. (1985). A Study of Factors Affecting Achievement Motivation. Unpublished Ph.D. Thesis (Psychology). Agra University, India.

Alanen, L. (1990). "Rethinking Socialization, the Family and Childhood," (pp. 12-28) in P.A. Adler, P. Adler, N. Mandell and S. Cahill (eds.), *Sociological Studies of Child Development: A Research Annual.* Volume 3. Greenwich, Connecticut/London: JAI Press.

Aries, P. (1962). *Centuries of Childhood. A Social History of Family Life.* New York: Vintage Books.

____. (1994) "Das kind und die Strasse- von der Stadt zur Anti-Stadt," in Philoppe Arie's (ed.) *Saint-Pierre oder die Susse des Lebens.* pp. 60–77. Berlin: Wagenbach.

Baldwin, A. (1979). "The Appraisal of Parent Behaviour," *Psychological Monographs,* 63 (4): 313.

Bardy, M. (1994). "The Manuscript of the 100-years Project: Towards a Revision," (pp. 299-317) in J. Qvortrup, M. Bardy, G. Sgritta and H. Wintersberger (eds.), *Childhood Matters. Social Theory, Practice and Politics.* Aldershot: Avebury.

Barrett, M. and M. McIntosh. (1982). *The Anti-social Family.* Thetjord: Verso.

Boocock, S.S. (1976). "Children in Contemporary Society," (pp. 414-436) in A. Skolknick (ed.), *Rethinking Childhood.* Boston: Little Brown and Co.

Boulding, E. (1999). *Children's Rights and the Wheel of Life.* New Brunswick, N.J.: Transactions Books.

Bredekamp, S. and C. Copple (eds.) (1977). *Developmentally Appropriate Practice in Early Childhood Programmes.* Washington DC: National Association for the Education of Young Children.

Bremback, C.S. (1966). *Social Foundation of Education: A Cross Cultural Approach.* New York: Johnweley and Sons Inc.

Castro, L.R. (1996). "The Time of Childhood: Or When 'Now' Becomes 'Not Yet'," (pp. 67-80) in G. Pfeffer and D.K. Behera (eds.), *Contemporary Society: Childhood and Complex Order.* New Delhi: Manak Publication Ltd.

____. (2000). "Children in Cities: Un-invited Participants," *Journal of Social Sciences,* 4 (2-3): 135-142.

Chinappan, G. (1987). Equalization of Educational Opportunities. Unpublished Ph.D. Thesis (Education). Poona University, India.

Clements, R. (2001). *Elementary School Recess.* Boston: American Press.

Cohen, P.C. (1996). "Children's Rights: The Changing International Legal Paradigm," in G. Pfeffer and D.K. Behera (eds.), *Contemporary Society: Childhood and Complex Order.* New Delhi: Manak Publications.

Ennew, J. (1991). "The Child as Social Actor," paper presented in the International Seminar on *Social Policies for Children and Adolescent,* Instituo degli Inocenti, Florence, Italy Februart, 22-23.

Epstein, J.L. (1995). "School/Family/Community Partnerships: Caring for the Children We Share," *Phi Delta Kappan,* 76 (9): 730-742.

Feldek, L. 1988. *Metafory.* Praha: Lovenska Krihovna, Ceskoslovenky Spisovatel.

Field, N. (1995). "The Child as a Labourer and Consumer. The Disapperance of Childhood in Contemporary Japan," (pp. 51-79) Sharon Stephans (ed.), *Children and the Politics of Culture.* Princeton: Princeton University Press.

Frones, I. (1994). "Dimensions of Childhood," (pp.145-164) in J. Qvortrup, M. Bardy, G. Sgritta and H. Wintersberge (eds.), *op. cit.*

Garrison, K.C. (1982). *Growth and Development.* New York: Longmans.

Giddens, A. (1979). *Central Problems in Social Theory: Action, Structure and Contradiction in Social Analysis.* London: Macmillan.

Goldscheider, F.K. and J.L. Waite. (1991). *New Families, No Families.* Berkeley: University of California Press.

Greenberg, P. (1989). "Parents as Partners in Young Children's Development and Education: A New American Fad? Why does it Matter?" *Young Children,* 44 (4): 61-75.

Gross, B. and R. Gross (eds.). (1977). *The Children Rights Movement.* New York: Anchor Press.

Hargreaves, A., L. Earl, S. Morre, and S. Manning. (2001). *Learning to Change: Teaching Beyond Subjects and Standards.* San Francisco, CA: Jossey-Bass.

Hartley, D. (1987). "The Time of their Lives: Bureaucracy and the Nursery School," (pp. 46-47) in A. Pollard (ed.), *Children and their Primary School.* London: Falmer Press.

Hengst, H. (1987). "The Liquidation of Childhood – An Objective Tendency," *International Journal of Sociology,* 17: 58-80.

Heredia, R.C. (1992). *Tribal Education for Community Development.* New Delhi: Concept Publishing Company.

Hughes, J. (1989). "Thinking About Children," (pp. 36-51) in G. Scaree (ed.), *Children, Parents and Politics.* Cambridge: Cambridge University Press.

Hungerland, B. (1999). "Childhood as a Product of Time Management," *Journal of Social Sciences,* 3 (1-2): 65-71.

James, A. and A. Prout. (1997). *Constructing and Reconstructing Childhood.* London: Falmer Press.

Kaplan, L. (1971). *Education and Mental Health.* New York: Harper and Row.

Katz, J. (1996). "The Rights of Kids in the Digital Age," *Wired*, 4th July.

Kirova-Petrova, A. (2000). Researching Young Children's Lived Experiences of Loneliness: Pedagogical Implications for Linguistically Diverse Students. *Alberta Journal of Educational Research,* 46: 99-116.

Kovaqik, J. (1994). "The Space and Time of Children at the Interface of Psychology and Sociology," (pp.101-122) in J. Qvortrup, M. Bardy, G. Sgritta and H. Wintersberger (eds.), *op. cit.*

Landsdown, G. (1994). "Children's Right," (pp.33-44) in B. Mayall (ed.), *Children's Childhood: Observed and Experienced.* London/ Washington DC: The Falmer Press.

Laslett, P. (1971). *The World We Have Lost* (2nd Edn.). Cambridge: Cambridge University Press.

Makrinioti, D. (1994). "Conceptualization of Childhood in a Welfare State: A Critical Reappraisal," in J. Qvortrup *et al.* (eds.), *Childhood Matters. Social Theory, Practices and Politics.* England: Avebury.

Matjcek, Z. (1985). "Jsou Nase Deti Pretezovancy?," (Are our Children Over-loaded?), *Psychologia a Patapsyologia Dietata,* 20 (6) : 92-114.

Mayall, B. (1994). "Children in Action at Home and School," (pp.114-127) B. Mayall (ed.), *Children's Childhood: Observed and Experienced. op. cit.*

Mead, M. (1930). *Growing up in New Guinea.* New York: Blue Ribbon.

Mehta, N. (2001). "Children's Right to Family: Promoting the Non-institutional Approach for Child Protection," *Perspectives in Social Work,* XVI (1): 260-287.

Meyer, P. (1983). *The Child and the State: The Intervention of the State in Family Life.* (translated by Janet Lloyd and Judith Ennew). London/New York/New Rochester/Melbourne/Sydney: Cambridge University Press.

Mishra, B.N. (1994). "Right to Copy," *The Prajatantra,* p. 14, Jan-7.

Mortier, F. (1997). "Competence in Children: A Philosophical Perspective," (pp. 99-144) in E. Verhellen (ed.), *op. cit.*

Nasman, E. (1994). "Individualization and Institutionalization of Childhood in Today's Europe," (pp.165-187) in J. Qvortrup, M. Bardy, G. Sgitta and H. Wintersberger (eds.), *op. cit.*

Nayar, U.S. (1991). "Labour of the Indian Girl Child: Multi-Curse, Multi-Abuse and Multi-Neglect," *The Indian Journal of Social Work,* LII (1): 37.

Oldman, D. (1994). "Adult-Child Relations," (pp. 43-58) in J. Qvortrup, M. Bardy, G. Sgritta and H. Wintersberger (eds.), *op. cit.*

Olmos, A. (1983). "Case Study of Swiss Migrant Joint Association CDSS Project 7," *The Education and Cultural Development of Migrants.* Strasbourg, France: Council of Europe.

Organization for Economic Co-operation and Development. (1997). *Parents as Partners in Schooling.* Paris: Author.

Patton, M.M. and J. Mercer. (1996). "Hey! Where is the Toys? Play and Literacy in 1st Grade," *Childhood Education,* 73: 110-116.

Phearman, L.T. (1969). "Comparison of High School Graduates Who Go to College with Those Who Do Not," *Journal of Educational Psychology,* 40: 405-414.

Piaget, J. and B. Inhelder. 1979. *The Psychology of the Child.* New York: Basic Books.

Pillai, N.P. (1979). *Organizational Climate, Teacher Morale and School Quality,* IInd Survey of Education Research, Baroda.

Qvortrup, J. (1987). "Introduction," in J. Qvortrup (eds.), *The Sociology of Childhood.* A special Issue of *International Journal of Sociology,* 17 (3): 1-16.

Qvortrup, J. (1994). "Childhood Matters: An Introduction," (pp.1-23) in J. Qvortrup, M. Bardy, G. Sgritta and H. Wintersberger (eds.), *op. cit.*

Rengifo, A.L.M. (2003). Columbia: Playing to Learn. An Alternative for Rural Children," *Early Childhood Matters,* 101: 24-28.

Rosenholtz, C. (1985). *The Organizational Climate of Schools.* U.S. Office of Education, Washington.

Sachidananda and P. Singh. (1989). *Education and Disadvantaged.* New Delhi: Uppal Publishing House.

Sgritta, G.B. (1987). "Childhood Normalization and Project. The Sociology of Childhood," *International Journal of Sociology,* 17 (3): 256-274.

Shamger-Handelman, L. (1994). "To Whom Does Childhood Belong?" (pp.249-265) in J. Qvortrup, M. Bardy, G. Sgritta and H. Wintersberger (eds.), *op. cit.*

Srivastav, A.K. (1985). "Social Class and Parent-Child Relationship in Urban Setting," *Eastern Anthropologists,* 38 (1): 19-52.

Sternberg, K.J., M.E. Lamb, C.D. Greenbaum, S. Dawud, R.M. Cortes, O. Krispin and F. Lorey. (1993). "Effect of Domestic Violence on Children's Behaviour Problems and Depression," *Developmental Psychology,* 29: 44-52.

Stone, L.J. and J. Chruch. (1966). *Childhood and Adolescence. A Psychology of the Growing Person.* New York: Random House.

Straus, M.A. (1994). *Beating the Devil Out of Them: Corporal Punishment in American Families.* San Francisco: New Lexington Press.

Straus, M.A., D.B. Sugarman and Giles-sims. (1997). "Corporal Punishment by Parents and Subsequent Anti-Social Behaviour of Children," *Archives of Pediatrics and Adoloscent Medicine,* 155: 761-767.

Thompson, C. (1969). *It's Adequacy, Problems and Needs.* New York: Harper and Bros.

Thorne, B. (1987). "Re-visioning Women and Social Change: Where are the Children?" *Gender and Society,* 1 (1): 85-109.

UNICEF. (1992). *Convention on the Rights of the Child.* Manila: UNICEF.

Verhellen, E. (1994). *Convention on the Rights of the Child.* Leuven/Apeldoorn: Garant Publishers.

Wartofsky, M. (1981). "The Child's Construction of the World and the World's Construction of the Child: From Historical

Epistemology to Historical Psychology," (pp.188-223) in F.S. Kessel, and A.W. Seigel (eds.), *The Child and other Cultural Inventions.* New York: Praeger.

Wirth, L. (1995). "The Problem of Minority Groups," (pp. 347-372) in R. Linton (ed.), *The Science of Man in the World Crisis.* Columbia/New York: University Press.

Young, P.V. (1996). *Scientific Social Survey and Research.* (3rd Edn.) Bombay: Asia Publishing House.

Zinnecker, J. (·1990). "Vom Strassenkind zum Verhauslichten kind. Kindheitsgesc hihte im Prozess der Zivilisation," in Imbke Behnken (Hrsg). *Stadtgesellschaft und kindheit im Prozess der Zivilisation:* 142–162. Opladen: Leske + Budrich.

Index